ONE MARRIAGE TWO FAITHS

Guidance on Interfaith Marriage

By

JAMES H. S. BOSSARD

and

ELEANOR STOKER BOLL

THE RONALD PRESS COMPANY · NEW YORK

Library of Congress Catalog Card Number: 57–6823

To
THE MANY MEN, WOMEN, AND CHILDREN
WHO HAVE SHARED WITH US
THEIR EXPERIENCES IN INTERFAITH MARRIAGES

Preface

In all our years of advising, teaching, and research in field of family relationships, we have found few subjects more frequently raised by puzzled men and women than the problem of interfaith marriages. Again and again we have been asked advice by husbands and wives; again and again we have heard from young people of the difficulties they had as children in homes where the parents were of different religious faiths.

It was to meet the questions and problems of such people that we decided to write this book. We have been gathering case histories for a quarter of a century and more, collecting information from parents, relatives, children, and grandchildren as well as from the couples themselves. Many of these family histories cover twenty or more years; some cover a generation and longer; in a few cases, four generations are included.

The present book is squarely based on this first-hand case material. We are concerned only that the reader should see for himself, from actual examples, how important a part religion can play in the whole way of life of an individual and how difficult marital adjustment can be with a partner of widely different religious background. Our approach is not one of admonition, advocacy, denunciation, or despair. It is factual, designed to give honest insight and concrete help to those contemplating interfaith marriages or already involved in them.

Any final verdict on a particular mixed marriage must rest with the people personally concerned in it. But we hope we have presented, clearly and concisely, the factors that must be weighed before an intelligent decision can be reached.

James H. S. Bossard
Eleanor S. Boll

Philadelphia

Contents

ONE MARRIAGE
TWO FAITHS

CHAPTER ONE

Marriage in America

Most persons marry or expect to do so. This is particularly true in the United States at the present time. We Americans are the most married people in the world. Our marriage rate is customarily the highest in the world. Similarly, in the proportion of the population fifteen years of age and over that is married, and in the percentage of those widowed and divorced who remarry, no other great nation compares with us. Currently, almost 70 per cent of the population fifteen years of age and over is married—the highest proportion in our history. We marry relatively early in life, and do so increasingly. We rush into marriage with greater haste and with fewer preparatory rituals than do most other people. Our standard of family living, in a material sense, is the highest in the world, and so, we are told, is our expectation of romantic happiness in marriage. When our marriages fail, and at least one out of every four now does, we rush into the next marriage with unabated abandon. Even widowhood is in a relatively large number of cases but a prelude to another marriage.

One of the most striking facts about marriage in this country is the extent to which persons from widely different backgrounds mate with each other. Our young people, and older ones too, are constantly crossing economic, social, and religious lines in their marriages, and we have come to accept this as part of the American creed of tolerance and social opportunity. Marriages between persons of differing religious faiths form a large part of these marriages. Recent studies show that as many as one half, and in certain cases an even larger proportion of the members of selected large religious bodies, are marrying persons outside of their faith. Moreover, the percentage of such cases has been increasing ever since the opening years of the twentieth century.

There are many reasons for the large and increasing number of interfaith marriages. Mixed marriages result from a mixed population, and, as everyone knows, our population is made up of many diverse elements, recruited from every corner of the globe. This is a process that has been going on in varying degrees throughout our history, and since 1820 we have had fairly reliable information on its extent. Combining the 19th century from that date on and the first half of the 20th century, a total of 39,325,482 immigrants were admitted legally into the United States. We have emphasized the fact of legal admissions, for it is well known that the smuggling of immigrants into this country has been a time-honored form of law violation.

It is important to note here that the major part of this inflow occurred within a single generation. In 1890 the population of the United States was, in round numbers, 63,000,000. Then from 1890 to 1924, a period of 34 years, 22,500,000 immigrants were admitted legally into the United States—a mass movement with few if any parallels in human history. Nor is it the size of the movement alone which is so outstanding. By the nineteen twenties when the major influx was lessening, more than 30 different national origin groups were represented in goodly size in our population. Obviously we have here, as a backdrop for the study of mixed marriages, as well as for many other major problems, one of the outstanding facts of recorded history, and it is a curtain, like Joseph's coat, made up of many colors.

Each of these many elements has brought its own ways of living and thinking, its language and customs, its mores and religion, and such is the freedom which this country permits that each group has been allowed to retain and exercise freely its own ways and values. In fact, not only has there been freedom to retain, but each element has been encouraged to make its contribution to the common heritage.

Faced with this unique and magnificent freedom, many newcomers quickly changed to conform to the American pattern. This has been particularly true in regard to many of the externals of personal appearance and public conduct. Other less tangible aspects of their national and racial past have been more persistent. Chief among these have been language and religion, the latter being the most persistent of all.

What has been happening during the past generation is quite obvious. The large numbers of immigrants that arrived during the generation after 1890 have now become established and have gravitated toward conformity to the common pattern in many aspects of life, mingling freely with other elements in the population, yet retaining some of the more deeply imbedded intangibles in their private lives. Foremost among the ones retained are those which grow out of and are influenced by religious connections.

It is out of this background that the problem of interfaith marriages grows. Young people of all elements, meeting in the come-and-go relations of school, play, work, and national service, seeing the conformity to the common externals of life, tend to marry without reference to the less obvious intangible differences between them. Chief among these less tangible differences are those of traditional religious faith.

There are other factors rampant in American life which accentuate this problem. One of these is the mobility of our population. The American people do not stay put. As characteristic as movement into this country from other lands have been internal movements from one place to another— east to west, south to north, country to city, interior to sea coast, city to suburb. Millions of persons cross state lines each year in search of jobs. At any one time, more than one-fifth of all native-born citizens are living in states other than those in which they were born. Thirty million Americans changed their residence during World War II days. Mobility is particularly evident in large scale studies of children, which show that, in the age group 7 to 13 years, more than a third already live in places other than where they were born. The life of many an American child today is one of movement from one neighborhood, one school, one play group, to another, each move increasing their exposure to and increasing their contacts with young people with other backgrounds and heritages.

Whatever the other consequences of mobility of population may be, it clearly is disruptive of family solidarity. Mobility tends to emphasize the immediate family over against the more extended kinship type. The role of grandparents, uncles, and aunts lessens as the distance between them and the immediate family increases. Their counsel is less sought and followed. Clearly, this is a fertile setting for the next factor important in this connection.

Marriages in this country are largely made on the basis of

the personal choice of the young people. It is they who are being married, not their parents or relatives, they point out. They have been educated to the American creed of personal rights and individual development; theirs, therefore, is the sole right to choose. And the basis of the choice is love, romantic love. Isn't this what the Hollywood movies, the novels, the plays continually emphasize? What matter then these other things that older people talk about? Isn't this the brave New World, with freedom to love, to choose, to marry whom you please?

And what about the advice and admonition of pastor, priest, or rabbi? What if the church counsels caution? Well, marriage is just as legal if performed by a justice of the peace. Marriage is a legal contract, isn't it? What right does the church have to interfere with our happiness? Ours is a secular society, they have been told. And a secular society means the rejection of the old, the traditional, the tried, the true, the time honored. And this in turn means the acceptance of new ways of thought, new values, new beliefs, evolved on the basis of free and open criticism, discussion, and scientific analysis. So cries modern youth, ignoring the accumulated wisdom of the ages. Our own choice in marriage, and for love: this is the secular age in marriage and family life.

In the preceding pages we have sketched briefly the main developments in American life which have given us a large and increasing proportion of interfaith marriages. Considered in terms of these underlying factors, there is nothing strange or mysterious or unnatural about such marriages; on the other hand, an explanation of their source is not in any sense a justification or defense of them. Actually, the defense or encouragement of such marriages comes from a relatively few persons, other than those who participate in them. Other comments are frankly critical, openly doubtful, or hestitant and lukewarm at best.

One fact is clear. Interfaith marriages do present personal and family difficulties of varying kinds and degrees which cannot be waved away by the magic wand of wish. They appear regardless of the professed attachment of those involved to their respective churches. They appear for the agnostic and atheist, the skeptic and the emancipated as well, for these too are professions of faith. And the difficulties involved need to be faced, and appraised, before entering into what it is hoped will be a lifelong union. Certainly there is nothing to be lost by doing so; and quite possibly something can be gained. For the stakes are high—personal happiness, relations with parents and kinsfolk, the happiness and best interests of the children that are to be.

We do not imply, either here or in any part of the discussion that follows, that mixed marriages are the sole or even of necessity the main key to family difficulties and tensions. As we shall emphasize in Chapter 3, the factors which break up marriages are many and varied, and differences in religious affiliations and faiths are but one of these.

The earnest purpose of this book is to consider how such differences tend to affect family living and child development. It is not written to denounce or to encourage such marriages. It presents the viewpoint of no particular church or creed. It is a book which has grown out of the professional work and research studies of the authors, both of whom have spent a generation (and more in point of time) working in the field of family relations and child development. During these years no problem has been presented to them more frequently for counsel; certainly few problems in marriage are more fundamental, persistent, and stubbornly pervasive.

In the next chapter we shall give concrete examples of what interfaith marriages actually involve, and then, in succeeding chapters, we shall look at their implications in more complete details, as well as present the established policies of the leading church bodies toward such marriages. Always, throughout the volume that follows, it is our purpose to help the reader to understand, believing that honest understanding is always of some help.

CHAPTER TWO

They Married Outside Their Faith

Perhaps the best way to begin a discussion of interfaith marriages is to do so concretely, that is, to tell in brief and simple fashion the stories of some persons who have married outside their faith. Here, then, are six case histories of such marriages, selected from a large collection of histories of mixed marriages which we have gathered through the years. These particular cases are chosen because each shows some one outstanding feature or problem that recurs over and over again among our case histories.

x 1. The first case tells in part the experience of two intelligent young people, both college graduates, who contracted an interfaith marriage with the buoyant confidence of youth that love and broadmindedness could overcome all obstacles.

There were many reasons why Edna and Frank expected to be very happy in their marriage. Both were intelligent and well educated. They were graduates of the same college and had majored in the same subject. Frank had been a campus big wheel and had been active in his fraternity. Edna had been president of her sorority. In disposition they were well suited to each other. Each had a keen sense of humor and some capacity to be objective about themselves and their problems. That Frank was a Roman Catholic and Edna a Presbyterian was well known to their friends, but those who thought seriously about this difference believed it to be relatively unimportant, since both were "liberal minded" and "reasonable" and would be sure to take "in stride" any problem that might arise.

Ten years after their marriage, Edna, from whom this story was obtained, recalled how "little clouds" had appeared the first months of their marriage in spite of the most auspicious beginnings. Frank obtained promising employment, and with some financial help from both families they started housekeeping on their own from the very start of their married life. Theirs had been an invalid marriage in the eyes of Frank's church because it had been performed by the Protestant chaplain of their college and without the guarantees that the Catholic church requires for a valid mixed marriage.

The first "cloud" came with Edna's discovery that Frank assumed, as the male's prerogative, that they would go regularly to the Catholic church, as a matter of course, and that if he accompanied Edna to the Presbyterian church it was a kind of graciousness on his part. Edna frankly admitted that she had made similar assumptions on her part.

Next, Edna came to resent a certain smirking smile on Frank's part, whenever they attended the Presbyterian church, over the informalities of its procedure. On her part, she says she tried conscientiously to enter into the spirit of the Catholic service, but it was all so very strange to her.

When, a year after their marriage, a daughter was born to them, the first definite clashes occurred. Frank wanted the child to be born in the local Catholic hospital, which had an excellent reputation. Edna insisted on the Presbyterian hospital, and when her mother came to be with her in the days immediately before the birth of the child the two joined forces to win their point.

Soon the question of the daughter's baptism arose. Frank wanted her to be baptized in the Catholic church. Edna, with a Presbyterian minister for a grandfather, and with a baby daughter, insisted that she be baptized by the Presbyterian minister. Frank was definitely displeased but finally capitulated. Eighteen months later a son was born, and now it was Frank that was insistent, and now it was Edna who came around to his point of view.

It was at this time that the question of birth control became an issue. Edna pointed out that with two children to support, and with high standards for their education, contraceptive methods were in order. Frank said little at first, but gradually began to bring forth the customary Catholic arguments against it. Soon Edna took matters into her own hands, and contraceptive devices began to be used.

Matters rested thus for a time, with some underlying tension which slowly, subtly began to interfere with their enjoyment of the marital relationship. When the older of their children neared the age of four, Edna decided that, as soon as this daughter went to kindergarten, she would like to take graduate courses at the nearby university, looking toward a Master of Arts degree. Frank countered with the plea that they have more children. The whole problem was resolved finally on a compromise. Edna would take her Master's degree, she would have her way in the use of contraceptives, then after the degree was obtained there would be more children.

Meanwhile, the question of the choice of the children's school arose. Frank pointed out the nearness of a parochial school, but Edna insisted that their daughter go to public school. Two years later, their son was enrolled in the parochial school. This decision carried forward a kind of compromise with children of mixed marriages which is common in certain European countries—the sons following the religion of the father and the daughters that of the mother.

One result of this division became increasingly apparent as the children's schooling proceeded. Different schools meant different companions and friends, different school events, different interests, many of them of a pervasive kind. By the time the children were in the third and fifth grades, respectively, this cleavage began to be noticeable to both parents.

Edna won her Master's degree in scheduled time, and a year later gave birth to a second son, only to find that the same problems remained—of the son's baptism, schooling, contraception after a time, and so forth.

Ten years after her marriage, Edna spoke feelingly of her experience. She loved Frank, she was sure Frank loved her. She said that Frank was a good provider for his family, was a good husband and father, and was a reasonable person. If only there were not these stubborn, insoluble differences between them, "ours would be a perfect marriage. Frank tries to see my viewpoint, but it's the way he was brought up. And I come from a long line of Presbyterians. As it is, we sort of limp along from one near crisis to another."

✓ 2. The case that follows is that of another Protestant-Catholic marriage. It reveals the deep emotional reactions of two young people who made an ill-advised marriage, with the religious difference its most obvious aspect. A number of years of bitterness, unhappiness, and fear resulted, changing materially the lives of both.

Dale, the only daughter of a successful professional man, was the apple of her father's eye. The family lived south of the Mason and Dixon Line. Her home was one of refinement —music, books, plays, the opera. As she grew up, she read a great deal and did well in her studies, so that when, after her coming-out party, she decided to enroll in a nearby college everyone thought it was just what she should do.

In her second year at college, she took a course in which there was much discussion of the different elements in the American population and the problem of their relation to each other. The teacher was popular with the students, and Dale, who projected the respect she had for her father upon her instructors, was much impressed by this teacher's enthusiasm and idealism. So, when he argued for intermarriage as a requirement of the great American melting pot at work, it all seemed very clear and proper to her.

It was just about this time that Dale met, on a blind date, a young Italian, also a student at the same college, but a year ahead of Dale. He was handsome, had a good line, and seemed to Dale a very dashing figure. Also, he was ardent, which to her seemed a pleasing contrast to the controlled poise of her well-mannered life. Date followed date, and Peter literally swept Dale off her feet. The fact that she was an Episcopalian and Peter a Roman Catholic seemed of no consequence at the time. Without a word to their families, they were married in mid-June, and Dale was so excited that she barely noticed the promises she made in order that the marriage might be valid in the eyes of Peter's church.

Shortly after their marriage, Dale went home to break the

news to her parents. They met the situation like the well-poised adults they were. Since Dale was married, she was told that her place was with her husband. When Dale intimated that she would like to continue her college studies, the parents indicated their willingness to give financial aid for that purpose. Dale went to live with her in-laws.

The realities of day-by-day living soon revealed the fundamental differences between Peter and Dale. First, there were the religious differences. Dale was a Protestant, an Episcopalian, accustomed since childhood to a very liberal-minded rector. Peter was a Roman Catholic, an ardent one, given to earnest observance of the requirements of his faith. Dale soon found that living in a devout Catholic family involved a whole series of observances and attitudes during the week, as well as the Sunday worship. Moreover, there were social differences which accentuated the religious ones. Dale had grown up on the right side of the railroad tracks; Peter had not. His family, while industrious and law-abiding, were "first-generation" people.

The matter of sex relations quickly became a problem between Peter and Dale. Dale was immature in many ways, not prepared to face motherhood. Moreover, she wanted to finish college. She insisted on the use of contraceptives; Peter hotly argued that they were married and that nature be allowed its sway.

By the end of August, Dale had returned to the home of her parents. Peter followed her, first entreating, then threatening her. Finally, his attitude was so menacing that Dale's parents asked him to leave. Repeated efforts at telephone communication followed. In September, Dale returned to college. Peter promptly appeared there and continued his tactics, gradually becoming more heated and threatening.

The first week in November, Dale had become so fearful that she withdrew from college and returned home.

A good deal of unpleasantness followed in the next eight months. Peter kept reappearing at Dale's home, asking to see "his wife." He and Dale met a number of times to talk things over. Dale first suggested a "cooling-off period" of separation. Peter insisted on his "rights" as a husband. Dale next suggested a divorce, to which Peter was violently opposed, indicating that he would never accept a divorce and would fight it legally at all times and in all places.

Late the following summer, Dale and her parents began to fear for her safety, and in early fall she fled with the utmost secrecy to live with a friend of her mother's in a city more than a thousand miles away from home. For security reasons, she adopted a fictitious name. Here she lived quietly for about two years, after which she moved to a western state and secured a divorce. Peter did not file an answer or put in an appearance. At the present writing, some six years have passed since the divorce, and Dale is happily remarried. She still has moments, however, when she becomes apprehensive over the possibility of Peter's reappearance in her life, although she is now living a goodly distance from the parental home. The entire experience has left deep psychological scars, and Dale sadly laments the years overshadowed by "her problem."

3. Our third case illustrates the fact that a marriage between persons of markedly different religious faiths may give for years the appearance of complete happiness, with the definite insistence of both parties that their marriage presents no problem, only to have it break at least one of them on the rocks of a submerged feeling of guilt.

One of the big difficulties in the study of life, according to an English philosopher of the nineteenth century, is the long span of time that often stretches between what we do and the final results of what we do. This was clearly the case in the marriage of Catharine and Solomon. Catharine was twenty-two when she met Sol at a Halloween party. The fact that she was a member of the Roman Catholic church and that he was reared in an Orthodox Jewish family received but passing attention from both. Catharine was intriguing to look at, pert in manner, and strongly attracted to this tall, handsome Jew. Perhaps the attraction between them was largely physical: both were healthy, vigorous persons, and the response of each to the other was markedly strong. Neither paid more than scant attention to the remonstrances of their families and friends. Ten weeks after their first meeting, they were married by a City Clerk.

As time went on, Catharine often spoke to her friends of her happiness, always in very positive terms. "My husband is a Jew, and the Jewish men make the best husbands." In fact, Catharine spoke of this so often and so positively that once a psychiatrist, visiting Catharine and Solomon one evening, remarked to his wife on their way home: "Methinks this lady does protest a little too much." Sol, too, was equally enthusiastic through the years. "My wife," he would say, "is a Catholic, and anything that she is, is good enough for me."

In the years that followed, no problems resulting from the difference in their faiths seemed to arise. Catharine ceased to go to church; Solomon had never been given to attendance at the Temple, and he now no longer observed any of the rites and holidays of his people. The two were devoted to each other, and proudly proclaimed the fact to their friends and families. Three years after their marriage, a daughter, Marie, was born, still further cementing their devotion to each other. The daughter was reared without church connections, so that here again the problem that is so troublesome in many marriages of this kind did not arise.

The twenty-fifth anniversary of their marriage coincided with the graduation of their daughter from college, and the two events were celebrated with a gala party. Catharine beamed and, as she had done consistently for twenty-five years, spoke of their great happiness. Husband and daughter joined to complete the picture of the happy family. Here, one thought, is a mixed marriage that has presented no problems.

It was in the twenty-sixth year of their marriage that tragedy began casting its shadows. First came a serious home accident, as a result of which Catharine's right arm was mangled. Weeks of hospitalization followed, during which the injury healed but the hand and a part of the arm were lost. Scarcely was she settled in her home when Marie was injured in an automobile accident, resulting in a broken leg and injuries to the spine which necessitated prolonged hospitalization.

Catharine found the succession of these two accidents very hard to bear. But the end was not yet. During the last week of Marie's stay in the hospital, Catharine's brother, the favorite brother, with whom she had kept the closest ties during the years, was shot accidentally by a gunman during a running fight between this gunman and the police. At this point, Catharine went to pieces completely. Within a few days she became a serious mental case.

Most significant in connection with the theme of this book is the form which Catharine's aberrations took. She seemed very sure that she was to blame for all these misfortunes, that they were all punishments sent by a long-suffering Deity for the sin which had been hers during all these years. After all, she would sob, she really had known better. She had been reared a good Catholic, and yet for all these years she had lived with a man without the sanction of her church. She had borne a child and had not reared her in the church; she herself had not attended for more than a quarter of a century. Small wonder that the patience of a long-suffering Deity had been exhausted and was now punishing her for her sins. Thus concluded Catharine.

One need not be an expert in the field of mental disturbances to realize that what was now happening to Catharine was a coming to the surface of a long-dormant sense of guilt. For years this had been buried deep in the layers of her unconscious self. Her constant insistence upon her happiness to all and sundry of her friends was but an effort to keep that sense of guilt from coming to the surface. It took the accumulated effect of three major misfortunes to weaken the resistance enough to let it break through.

4. The fourth case involves the marriage between two Protestants; yet the difference between the lives of the two families from which they stemmed, based on the requirements and permissions of their respective religions, was so great that here again the marriage broke one of the pair. This is a type of interfaith marriage that is generally overlooked but which, as we shall see, may be of very considerable importance.

Myra and Roger had known each other since they were in grammar school together. Their first meeting came about by chance when their teacher noticed that each of them had an unusually good singing voice. One day, while preparing a Friday afternoon program for the parents of the children, it occurred to the teacher to team them up in a singing duet. Their success was immediate and marked. Almost at once, they were asked to sing at a special service in the teacher's Sunday school, where they scored an even more impressive triumph.

Six years of singing together at school, church, and community affairs now followed. Sometimes these public appearances came as often as two or three times a week. All this required hours of rehearsing, sometimes at Myra's house, a few times at Roger's, and still other times at other places where facilities were available. Both were devoted to music and conscientious in their performances. As a result, most of the time they spent together was devoted to their musical interests, so that at the end of six years they had spent many hours with each other and yet knew remarkably little about each other in other aspects of their lives.

No one was surprised when, at the end of the sixth year of their singing together, they were married, nor did it occur to their families and friends to raise any doubts about the propriety of the marriage. Both were Protestants. He was a German Lutheran; she and her family were ardent members of a small sect commonly referred to locally as Holy Rollers.

Since Roger was only nineteen and out of high school but one year, the newlyweds went to live with Roger's people. In this household at the time there were three generations of German Lutherans. They were a happy, jovial lot. There was much beer drinking. During the Prohibition era, beer was brewed extensively within the home. Card games flourished nightly. Sundays were days of gala feasting and visiting.

To Myra, this way of life was highly unacceptable; in fact, it was downright sinful. In the home in which she had been reared, all such forms of recreation were taboo. Beer was Satan's brew. Cards were a device of the devil. The Sabbath was for prayer, meditation, and worship. At the time when young people in other churches were confirmed, Myra was "washed in the blood of the Lamb." As a "saved" person, she was dedicated to the avoidance of the evils which throve so blissfully in Roger's household.

After their marriage Roger began to lose interest in their singing. He had his living to make, he said, and it was true that his job required more and more of his time, including evenings away from home. At first Myra would "escape" from "Roger's people's home," as she put it, by visiting her own folks. But soon a succession of events eliminated this opportunity. First, her mother died, and five months later her father was killed accidentally while at work. Slightly more than three months later, her brother, the only other child, married and accepted employment almost a thousand miles away. A year after her marriage to Roger, she had, as she put it, no home, no people, no place to go to but with Roger's people.

Myra hoped desperately for a child during these months. A baby, she thought, would make such a difference. Then Roger and she would leave his folks' home and have one of their own. Timidly, she began to suggest this to Roger, but he, preoccupied with his job, showed little interest in such a move. After all, he argued, life in this happy household is pleasant, and financially it is very economical. It is obvious that Roger's dependence upon his family, his unwillingness to cut the parental ties and go with Myra on their own, complicated the whole situation.

As Roger's reluctance to develop a home of his own became more and more clear to Myra, her eagerness for a child turned to a feeling of cold fear. Suppose I did have a child, she thought, would I want to rear it with these beer-drinking, card-playing, roistering people? No, no, never. Far better not to have a child, her reason dictated. But I am a woman, I want a child, children, like other women. A year passed, and another. Myra became thin, pale, nervous. "She needs to loosen up and have some fun," said Roger's folks, but the more they urged this the more Myra shrank within herself.

In her unhappiness, Myra turned to a former classmate whose husband was just beginning the practice of medicine. "You need a tonic," said the young doctor. "Get out in the sunlight. Get as much fresh air as you can." Myra agreed, but with very little enthusiasm. Three months later, she was back in the young doctor's office, having lost six more pounds from a body already too frail. "We must consult a specialist," said the doctor. "I know just the man."

The great specialist finally faced her in his office. He had been studying the reports of the tests he had ordered. "Humph. Nothing physically wrong. We must tone up your system. I tell you what I want you to do. I want you to go to Lukens Riding Academy. You know where that is? I want you to go horseback riding, at least three times a week."

Myra's death several years later was not a sudden event. The last pulse of life was like the slow spiral fall to earth of the last leaf of a now bare tree. Myra had died spiritually some time before. "Those Gloster people [Myra's family] all were queer," said Roger's people. "But she was sweet, and such a good singer," said Roger.

5. One of the crucial points about any interfaith marriage is its meaning for the children born to such unions. This is a very important area. The range of problems presented, and their far-reaching consequences in the developing lives

of the child members of these families, constitutes a distinct challenge to all those persons who are interested in children and their wholesome development.

George was a junior in high school when he first met Ethel. Although he and all of his family were Roman Catholics, he had not gone to Catholic schools since the eighth grade when his father had been displeased with their treatment of George. Apparently the change from the parochial to the public school was a satisfactory one for George, for he made a quick and satisfactory adjustment to the public school system. By the time he was a junior, he was on the varsity basketball team and stood well in his studies.

Ethel's family had come from the South, and she entered high school in her sophomore year. Her warm and friendly nature, her comely appearance, and her southern drawl speedily won her full acceptance in the high school life.

George and Ethel were drawn to each other almost at once. They were in the same sections in English and History, they enjoyed dancing with each other, and, in their senior year, both won a place in the cast of the annual senior play. After rehearsal they would always go home together, and after basketball games Ethel would always wait for George.

That George was a Catholic and Ethel a southern Baptist had little or no meaning for them: their hearts were young and gay and too full of the zest of life to think seriously about church differences. In the two years that followed graduation from high school, their lives were full of interesting experiences—jobs, athletics for George, and amateur theatricals for both.

The night after George proposed, and was accepted, he made some mention of the fact that they would have to be married in his church, and that she would have to sign some old paper to satisfy the priest. At least, so it sounded to starry-eyed Ethel, who scarcely heard him as she in turn promised to do what was necessary so they might be married.

Two years after a June wedding of two young people very much in love with each other, they had their second child. With the coming of the children, the happy couple began to face graver responsibilities than politely attending church with each other. Ethel found herself facing the formal agreement which she had signed—to rear her children in the Roman Catholic faith. This was no easy matter, particularly since both children "took" in appearance after her side of the house. Moreover, there were her parents, her brother, and two sisters with whom to contend. True, they were a happy, easy-going, tolerant family, but they were "southern Baptists from away back," and the southern Baptist way of life seemed the only proper and logical one.

But there were also George's folks. While they were not the most devout of Catholics, and in some matters were even critical of the church, they assumed that the children would be reared as Catholics, since the matter had been formally agreed upon before the wedding. Besides, was not George their father? The family assumed the inherent dominance of the male in important domestic matters. Fortunately, they had moved recently to another city some ninety miles away, which simplified matters to some extent for the time being.

First Ethel and then George became increasingly distressed over their problem. They were deeply devoted to each other, but the situation seemed insoluble. Finally, they agreed on a compromise. They would give the children a dual religious education. Having been baptized in the Ro-

man Catholic church, they would receive the same rite as
Baptists. Furthermore, they would attend both churches on
alternate Sundays.

All went well with this arrangement for several weeks.
Then George's father, having received a substantial increase in salary, asked that George and the whole family
spend every other weekend at the paternal home, the trip
to be made always at the grandparents' expense. George
and Ethel fitted the two schedules together. One Sunday
they visited Ethel's family and went with them to the Baptist church; the next Sunday, they journeyed to George's
parents' home and all went to the Catholic church. Neither
set of grandparents was told the full details of this dual arrangement.

This might have worked out as a satisfactory solution,
but children have a way of growing, of noticing, and of
talking. At first, George and Ethel would interpret the
slips the children made in conversation, but this created a
very tense situation for George and Ethel, and would only
mean a temporary avoidance of the issue. As time went on,
the children became increasingly puzzled, not only over the
differences in the services of the two churches but with
many details in the lives of the two sets of grandparents, as
well as the attitude of their parents. On the Baptist Sunday,
there was no card playing, no "unseemly" amusement, no
drinking of beer, only quiet, sober observance of the day.
The next Sunday, having gone to Mass, games and gaiety
were in order in the home of George's parents.

A double life, as it were, a dual set of standards, two sets
of teachings in an area which was emphasized as of the
greatest importance in life—these were the continuing experience, certainly of the children, and also of George and
Ethel. Seven years after their marriage, two young parents

and two very attractive children were living in a state of confusion, tension, and uncertainty. Under other circumstances, this might have been a very happy family. As things stand, their future as a family is uncertain.

6. Finally, we present the story of a marriage between a Pennsylvania Quaker and his Russian Orthodox bride, to call attention to the problem of the parents of a couple making a mixed marriage. This, too, is an important area, often as tragic as the frequency with which it is overlooked. In this case there was the particularly poignant confusion and mystification of the bride's parents over the strangeness of the particular marriage ceremony.

The two-hundred-year-old Quaker meetinghouse stood stark on the rural hillside in southeastern Pennsylvania. The early June sun was warm, but a cool breeze made it a pleasant Saturday afternoon. It was almost two o'clock: the last guests were being seated on the hard benches in the unadorned room. It was well because promptly on the stroke of two, the spirit moved all and sundry to a deep and eloquent silence. Seated in a prescribed pattern sat the bride and groom, their respective families, the members of the Meeting, and a handful of guests.

For some minutes, perhaps five, perhaps it was ten, no one spoke; there was none that stirred. Least of all the father of the groom. To him, this silence and all that followed were wholly familiar and proper. There, in this meetinghouse, he and Martha had been married twenty-six years ago; and before them, his parents, and his parents' parents. Here, in the adjoining burial ground, they now lay, marked by a headstone in size and design like all other headstones there. These were his people, this was his meetinghouse. And it was Martha's, too. True, her people were of lesser substance, but she too was a "birth-right" Friend. Martha and he had grown up together, they had gone to this meetinghouse, to the same Friends school, and had the same "concerns" as they had grown up. But now the silence is broken. The spirit has moved. The bridal pair arise, and, in formal words which are simple and which have been carefully memorized, *they marry themselves*. And then again that same stillness.

Stephanie, the bride, unlike the groom, was not a birthright Friend. She was not even a member of the Meeting. She had been born in Russia, and had been reared in the Russian Orthodox church. Seated near her were her parents. They had come from Chicago for the wedding of their only daughter, who, oddly enough, was being married in the groom's church. Again the silence is broken. Someone rises and hands the bridal pair a document which both sign. Then another person arises and recites in legal phraseology who it is that has been married.

The silence is resumed. The face of Dimitri, the father of the bride, seems to reflect a puzzled confusion. A wedding, but there is no holy edifice! Certainly this simple, unadorned room on a lonely hillside cannot be a church, he thought, and most assuredly not of a devout or substantial people. There was not even a priest, there were no holy vestments. There had not even been the customary invitation to the wedding. He recalled how, when he and his Ileana were married, they had gone about the community to make personal invitations to their friends.

Dimitri looked at the groom's father and mother. Now that the wedding would be celebrated at their house, why were they here? He remembered how, in the old country, the bride's father and mother did not go to church, but remained at home, to cry, and to prepare the house for the celebration. He remembered how, at his own wedding, the best man had escorted his Ileana down the aisle, and how he had walked with the maid of honor. How beautiful his Ileana had been that day. How proud he had been to stand with her as the priest completed the ceremony and placed on their heads the little gold crowns which the best man and maid of honor had carried. Here there was no proud walk to the altar, no ceremony, not even a best man and maid of honor. This young man must be very friendless, and as for Stephanie, she was a stranger here. A voice breaks in on his memories. Someone has arisen and is reading from a book. No, it is not the Bible or a prayer book. It seems to be some things that different people, students perhaps, had written about marriage and the family.

He glanced at his good Ileana. She seemed not to be hearing, for she too was remembering: after she and Dimitri were married, how they had gone to her parents' home. The fiddler was still playing. He had been playing ever since she had started to dress for the ceremony. She knocked at the door, as was the custom. "Who is there?" someone asks. She gives her married name. "I know of no such person," replies the voice. The playful banter goes back and forth. Finally, she convinces the doorkeeper that there is such a person, and they enter to begin the merriment.

This time, when the silence is broken, everyone rises and leaves the meetinghouse, to repair to the groom's home. Dimitri and his wife were the last to rise. There had been no signal, other than the moving of the spirit to those who were members of the Meeting. Could this be a wedding? Was this all there would be? Oh yes, they would go to the groom's home, and no doubt the real wedding would take place there. Truly, these were strange people.

The reception that followed was brief. There were

cookies and tea. Families and friends conversed quietly. Dimitri looked about, wondering where the musicians might be hidden. And when will the dancing begin? He wet his lips, in anticipation of the liquors that were sure to come. Tea was all right while things got under way. He remembered his own wedding, how Ileana danced until her feet and back ached, and as for a few drinks, well, he remembered them too. A few drinks would help right now, especially with these somber people. They needed more than a few to liven them up, he thought. His eyes gleamed, but not for long. What was this? People were leaving, by twos and fours. A young man presented himself. "Your car is parked across the street," he told them, "but there is no need to hurry. The train for Chicago doesn't leave for another hour and a half."

Later that night, as the train roared across the Pennsylvania hills, Dimitri's face was a study in deepest thought. Slowly the pieces of the puzzle took form in his mind. The afternoon, that setting devoid of all religious traces, the absence of a priest, the simple declaration by his Stephanie and her friend, the peculiar lack of festive celebration afterwards, the hurried departure of the guests—yes, it was all very simple now. He had heard of things like this before. His Stephanie. A common-law wife. No marriage. Just a declaration of intent to live together. Slowly his hand sought that of his Ileana. He turned to her. "Better," he whispered, "that we should have stayed in the old country."

Late that night, Albert Southward, the historian, and his wife were going to bed. "Albert," said his wife, "thee has been very quiet all evening. Didn't thee like the wedding between those two young people?" He sat silent a moment. "Jane," he said, "it was no wedding between two young people. It was like a treaty between two different worlds."

These six cases present so many facets of marriages between persons of different religious faiths. They are intended to reveal, with the concreteness of reality, what may happen in such marriages. Are these six cases typical of what happens when people of different faiths marry? What is the real nature and difficulty in all mixed marriages? What is the outcome of such marriages? Do they lead to happiness or unhappiness? What do they mean for the children? How many such marriages are there? Is their relative number increasing or decreasing? Why do all religions oppose such marriages? Why is the opposition of the churches becoming more and more pronounced? If you have made such a marriage, is the situation hopeless? Have some marriages of this kind been successful? And, if so, why? What constructive steps may be taken? These and other questions will be considered and answered in the succeeding pages of this book.

CHAPTER THREE

What Interfaith Marriage Really Means

INTERFAITH MARRIAGES ARE OF MANY KINDS

Interfaith marriages, or mixed marriages, as they are more commonly called, are of many different kinds. Many people overlook this fact, thinking only of Protestants, Catholics, and Jews as the three main religions in this country. Actually, this is very much of an oversimplification, as is evident when we look more closely at each of the three.

Let us begin with the Jews. For several thousand years their religion has distinguished them from their neighbors, and during this time they have retained a basic unity in their beliefs. Nevertheless, many distinctions have arisen. Most Jews in the United States are descended from immigrants who came within the past century, and from many countries. As a result, national origin differences have appeared, those between Russian and German Jews being perhaps the most obvious. Then there are the Reformed and Orthodox Jews, as well as the conservative wing.

Or, consider the term Catholic. There are Roman Catholics and Greek Catholics. The term English Catholics is often applied to High Episcopalians. These are divisions which involve wide differences in faith, ritual, and tradition. Particularly strong, and of long standing, are the historical distinctions here, many of which go back for centuries. Reinforcing the religious differences are strong feelings of nationality. Thus, Roman Catholicism is to many Irish a symbol of their separation from the British. In fact, it has been said that the reason the Irish are so intensely Catholic is because the British are Protestant. There is, for example, the story of the Englishman who is reported to have said to the Irishman: "The only reason you Irish are Catholic is because we English are Protestant. Now, if we English had been Catholic, all you Irish would be Protestant." To which the Irishman replied: "Yes, and begorra, it's damned good Protestants we would have been."

Finally, there are the many denominations combined under the term Protestant. These include Baptists, Christian Scientists, Congregationalists, Disciples of Christ, Dunkards, Episcopalians, Jehovah's Witnesses, Lutherans, Mennonites, Methodists, Moravians, Quakers, Presbyterians, Reformed, Seventh Day Adventists, and Unitarians, merely to enumerate at random a partial list.

In the United States as a whole there were, at the time of the last religious census, a total of 265 different religious bodies. Some of these are small sects, but there were seventy distinct denominations with memberships of fifty thousand or more, and nineteen with memberships of a million or more.

If differences in religious faith and church membership are considered, then all of these distinctions must be recognized. In other words, the marriage between a Dunkard and a Lutheran may represent a "wider crossing" than one between an Episcopalian and a Roman Catholic.

THE REAL NATURE OF RELIGIOUS DIFFERENCES

What is the real nature of interfaith marriages? Why are parents, relatives, friends, churches, and students of marriage so uniformly opposed to them, or at least skeptical of their chances of success? Does it mean that these people are narrow-minded and guilty of an intolerance which we Americans are taught to shun?

Many young people are inclined to think so. They tend to look at religious distinctions in terms of differences in theological beliefs, forms of worship, and kinds of organization. Thus they will tell you that differences in religion are not very important in marriage. We are intelligent, broad-minded people, they will say or think. We have been taught to be tolerant. We are willing to respect each other's religion. Peter can go to his church, and I'll go to mine. Or, better still, we will go together to each other's church.

If beliefs and forms of worship were the only, or even the chief, differences between religions, such attitudes would be quite proper and would reduce the problems of mixed marriages to lesser importance. But this is not the case. Any religion that has any value and vitality extends its beliefs into deeds—observances, abstinences, good works; and the more vital the religion the more true this is. Also, the older the religion the more these expectations of conduct have hardened into strict requirements.

Moreover, these requirements come to cover a wide range. Some religions require a distinct form of dress for all believers, like the Amish and Mennonites; others, only for specialized types of service, like the clergy, monks, nuns, and so forth. Many religions reach over into the eating habits of people—no pork, fish on Friday, no food before Communion, fasting on certain days, dietary observances during Lent, and the like. In various ways, religion dominates the whole area of recreation. Holidays originate often as Holy Days, and these become focal points in the organization of leisure-time activities. Some churches frown upon various forms of amusement, such as card playing, dancing, theater-going, and the singing of songs that are considered appropriate only on certain days and occasions. The Sabbath is variously observed, not only in worship but in the whole range of life's activities.

Even more important than the forms of worship and the observances which different religions emphasize are the ways of thinking that result. Just as thought often leads to action, so it is equally true that we live ourselves into thought. This is particularly true in the earlier years of life. As children we grow up in families where particular ways of behaving are stressed, and required of us. This point may be made clear if we stop for a moment to consider one of the most important functions which the family serves in the rearing of its children. Home is the place to which the child brings his experiences with life, with other children, his teachers, adults, moving pictures, the things he sees and hears. It is here that, in endless ways and in varying degrees, these experiences are sifted, appraised, interpreted, and evaluated. Home is the lair to which the child retreats to lick his wounds, the stage to which he returns to parade the glory of his achievements, the refuge he finds in which to brood over his ill treatment, real or fancied. The home is the great experience-defining agency in our lives; for a time, it is the only one. It is only later that other agencies come to support, modify, or contradict it. It is, then, out of this living, learning, defining process that we develop our beliefs, our choices, our life values.

There are, of course, many sources of the ways of thinking and evaluating which distinguish us, but every reader will realize that many of them represent our particular religious background. And this, let it be added, may be quite as true of persons reared in families with only a nominal degree of allegiance to their church as in those who may be highly active and devout. Throughout this entire volume, we are using the term *religious faith* quite independently from church membership, church activities, or formal religious profession. Every reader can think at once of many persons who are deeply devout, with strong convictions regarding their behavior, who have, at least at the time, no nominal church connection. One can think, for example, as a Presbyterian without being carried on the rolls of any church of that denomination.

Moreover, these group attitudes and values may exist, and frequently do, without people's awareness of their origin. We hold this to be true, for example, and we say that is so, because they are self evident. What is less evident to us is that we think they are self evident because successive layers in our past experience, beginning in infancy, have made us think so.

To the contemporary reader, reared in an intellectual atmosphere in which Sigmund Freud is almost as well known as Winston Churchill, and theories of the lasting effects of early childhood conditioning are a commonplace in popular thinking, the continuing importance of religious influences in our lives will be recognized even though we say that we have severed our church connections. We now understand, and it is important in this connection that we do understand, that the adult man or woman, boastful of their freedom from old-fashioned inhibitions, proud of their devotion to science and secularized ways of thought, find in these later areas often but a new set of terms to rationalize and justify the ideas that hold over from their post infantile days.

It is true that we have been going through an era of secularization in which we have exchanged old gods for new, but it is also true that much of the so-called secularization has been but a setting up of old gods on new altars and dressing them up in new pastel shades. An old belief, restated in scientific terminology in a current book in a multicolored jacket, and read in a newly constructed ranch house with broad picture windows, is still an old belief. Each generation likes to boast of its freedom from the past, only to discover that the present is its unruly child. We are never as free from the past as we think we are. The present religious revival, evidencing itself in various ways and especially among younger people, is one illustration of this, and a particularly important one in connection with interfaith marriages.

Social scientists have been using a term to describe this continuity of life to which we have been referring. It is the word *culture*, and it is used by them, not in the popular sense of meaning polish or refinement, but to designate the ways of living and the ways of thinking of a people. Thus they speak of the culture of the Japanese people, the French culture, or the culture of the Burmese.

It is an apt summary, then, of what we have been saying in this connection, to point out that Judaism is not a form of worship in the temple but a distinct culture, with a long history of development and a wide range of characteristics. Roman Catholicism is a culture—that is, it is a way of doing and a way of thinking. Presbyterianism is a culture; and so on through all the established religions. Divisions within the main religious bodies, previously referred to, might be spoken of as subcultures.

What this means specifically is that every religion includes the following elements:

1. A system of beliefs about God, life, and man.
2. Established forms of worship.
3. A set of observances in the lives of its followers.
4. A number of attitudes, life values, and behavior judgments.
5. A conception of life, now and in the hereafter; the relative importance of the now and the hereafter; the purpose of life; and the role of unseen forces and factors in life.

Once this thought is grasped, it is clear that an interfaith marriage is not merely a union between two people who have been in the habit of going to, or professing allegiance to, some particular church. It means that it is a union of two different cultures, or to put it more exactly, the union of two different cultural products.

At this point, someone may argue: Well, aren't we constantly meeting, working, and associating with people who are the products of different cultures? This is true, but in the case of interfaith marriages two important facts need to be stressed. One is that culture is a very pervasive thing, penetrating into every phase of our lives. It reveals itself particularly in those intimate aspects of our lives that are fundamental in the marital relationship and, later on, in the rearing of children. The other fact is that marriage is the most inclusive, intimate, and pervasive relationship in life. It is also a highly emotional relationship, and it is expected to be a permanent one. The adjustments which marital partners have to make reach out into every aspect of life. This makes a mixed marriage a cultural union quite different from any other we may form.

THE ROLE OF RELIGION IN SEXUAL BEHAVIOR

One aspect of the cultural union and adjustment in marriage calls for special consideration, and that is sex. Most of the discussions of interfaith marriages speak of sex only as it pertains to the question of birth control, arising usually when one of the marital partners is a Roman Catholic. It is true that this is a big and urgent problem, but the role of sex in interfaith or in any kind of marriage is far broader than that of reproduction and contraceptive behavior. Sex is a very basic part of the marital relationship, with reproduction in a sense an incidental part of it. The sexual act is a form of marital behavior by which and through which the married pair develop, express, and enrich their emotional relationship to each other. What this means, among other things, is that the sexual responses of the marital partners to each other, their attitudes toward sex, their sense of its deeper meaning, all are extremely vital.

Now what is important in this connection is that our attitudes toward sex, and its role in marriage, are derived in part, and perhaps in very large part, from religious sources. The Kinsey studies offer considerable support for this contention. They show that religious factors have an effect among women upon the incidence of masturbation, premarital petting, and premarital coitus. Findings in regard to the rate of marital coitus appear to be negative, although there are some indications of slower and more restrained response in marriage of the more devout women.

More significant for the rate of marital coitus is the role

of the male, since he is the one who has most to do with its determination. Here the Kinsey data show not only the role of devoutness and religious affiliation in regard to the incidence of masturbation and premarital petting, but also that "marital intercourse is consistently affected by the degree of church affiliation."

These findings are the result of the statistical manipulation of a large number of cases, although Kinsey and his associates frankly admit that the number of cases in the separate religious groups is too small to be satisfactory. Moreover, they deal with aspects of sex behavior which can be counted and tabulated, like the frequency of particular sexual acts. True, such facts are indicative, but for other insight into attitudes, values, and emotional responses or repressions we must turn to look at the universal relationship between religion and sex.

The basic fact is that religious codes have always and everywhere been the main source of the social attitudes which represent the sex morals of a people. These codes have regulated in considerable detail the conditions under which coitus might occur, the times on the church calendar when it was forbidden, positions to be assumed, and various other aspects of the relationship. Moreover, many religious groups still look upon marital coitus as a concession to the wickedness that is innate in man. What other meaning could be given to the teaching that all persons are conceived in wickedness and sin, or upon all the restrictions that are placed upon coitus during certain seasons like Lent or selected fast days? Small wonder that Dr. Kinsey and his associates concluded that there is nothing in the English-American social structure which has had more influence upon present-day patterns of sexual behavior than the religious backgrounds of that culture.

To be sure, there is some considerable variation in the conception of sexual behavior from one religious group to another. Strict Orthodox Jewish code and narrow Catholic interpretations accept the reproductive philosophy of sex, which means that sexual relationships, even within marriage, which do not look to this fruition are morally wrong. The Protestant churches vary from an attitude similar to the Jewish-Catholic one just mentioned to those which interpret sexual activity in terms of the total social adjustment of the individual.

We have selected the sex relationship as one example of how differences in religious background may affect the relationship between husband and wife. The results of religious conditioning in other areas of life might be selected, but it should be clear by now that the union of diverse religious cultures in marriage is very fundamental and far reaching, radiating out to the family meals, its holiday and recreational life, the education of the children, and the privacy of the marriage bed. We are not in any way passing judgment upon these differences; we are simply stressing the fact that they exist, and that they are numerous, pervasive, and fundamental.

NATIONAL ORIGIN VARIATIONS IN THE RELIGIOUS CULTURE

Close study reveals other complications in interfaith or mixed marriages. We have already referred to national origin differences in the various religious groups which accentuate and reinforce their distinction from each other. American Roman Catholics may be of Irish, Italian, French, or Spanish descent, to name only the larger examples. Jews may be German, Russian, or Polish. Lutherans stem mainly from German or Scandinavian sources. Presbyterians often have a Scotch ancestry. Every reader is sure to have heard references to facts of this kind in the popular references to Irish Catholics, German Lutherans, Russian Jews, or Scotch Presbyterians.

These national variations within the larger religious groups are particularly important in this country because of the many ethnic elements in our population which have migrated to the United States at different times and with differing religious patterns. The following case shows how important these national origin differences can be. We have deliberately selected a case where the two persons are of the same religious faith, to reveal clearly the nature and operation of these national differences.

Loretta, an Italian Catholic, married George, an Irish Catholic. They were both devout Catholics. They were both native-born children of foreign-born parents. They were in love. They were both very stable family people. They were not the results of the difficult type of conflict situations within their families. Though each of them still lived, at the time of their engagement, with their families in communities of respective Irish Catholics and Italian Catholics, they had lived in a well-adjusted setup. The homes of their parents were partly assimilated—sticking to many of the Irish and Italian customs, but never hindering their children in assimilating into American ways. They had assimilated. They had both gone through the public high schools and both had well-paying, semiskilled jobs.

There were no overt parental objections to their marriage, but both Loretta and George sensed a certain antagonism between their parents. They did not like each other. They did not feel comfortable with each other. Loretta said, "They acted as if my parents were not good enough for them." George said, "Loretta's family always thought my family was immoral."

Before they were married, Loretta and George had only one outspoken difficulty. Each one wanted to start house-keeping in the neighborhood in which he had formerly lived. Both neighborhoods were located within reasonable distance of the places where they worked. Loretta won out, and they moved into a small house close to where her parents lived.

Within a year, Loretta's face began looking very pinched and drawn. She was obviously highly nervous. Before long she broke out with the story. "There isn't anything that pleases him. He doesn't like it that I see so much of my Mother. He says that I'll never stop being a Wop if I live so close to my family. He doesn't like the parish we live in because most of us are of Italian descent and a parish like this, and its church, really *is* different from the one he is used to. He doesn't like the way we fuss over each other in our family. He says we are emotional. His family is, too, but they take it out in swearing at each other. We never swear in our family. He complains about my cooking. And I try so hard. He says I never cook anything but that damned spaghetti. I do cook spaghetti because I love it. But I have always tried to cook Irish dishes as often for him. But he says that I don't know how to cook them right. I guess I don't. His mother won't teach me how—and I just don't like them anyway. But I do try. We fight about drinking, too. We don't have anything against drinking, but he never drinks wine. Wine is best. You should drink it with your meals, and it acts slow and makes you feel kind. He only wants whiskey, straight, and whiskey raises the devil in you and makes you mean. I try to get him to come over to Momma's because I think she could make him see. But Momma isn't good enough for him."

At this point, Loretta was about ready to leave George and go back to her family—but, she discovered that she was pregnant. For a short time, differences were forgotten in the excitement of the prospect of having a child. But almost immediately, things began to get worse. Loretta's "emotional" family entered the picture more and more, now, with little things for the baby, suggestions about what Loretta should do during pregnancy. They were fluttery, and protective, and excited. This irritated George unbearably. George's parents were excited, too, in their own way. Their way seemed gruff, hard, and even ribald to Loretta. George felt that he would never stand to have Loretta's family "mushing" over his baby, and Loretta that she would not let her child be influenced by George's foul-mouthed relatives.

It was Loretta's mother who made a firm attempt to help out the situation. She told Loretta that since there was a child on the way there could be no separation, and that, since George was so unhappy where they were living, Loretta should try to live in a neighborhood more satisfactory for George. They then moved near George's parents.

It was a noble attempt. But, in this neighborhood, where George was constantly surrounded by his own old friends and old haunts, he became more completely what it was his natural heritage to be. It also made Loretta stick out like a sore thumb in the neighborhood. She, therefore, spent more and more time, while George was away, with her own family. Steadily and consistently, they drew apart. On the night that the baby was born, George took Loretta to the hospital and then departed, only to be brought back forcibly by his family. He was three sheets to the wind, and when he arrived, Loretta's whole family was there. The two families carried on in noble cooperation during that night, getting George sobered up and themselves celebrating the birth of their first grandchild in both families. But this was their last act of cooperation.

A child was born. To George and his parents, it belonged to them. To Loretta and hers, to them.

It became a point with each parent to accentuate his own cultural survivals, in order to keep the child free from those of the other parent.

These people had difficulties in their personal adjustments, obviously. But, the fact is that their personality difficulties were so stressed by cultural differences that there was never any opportunity to get down to the level of plain personality adjustment. They, their families, their whole cultural heritages were constant irritations, which they seized upon, and about which they rationalized, in order to avoid any really sincere analysis of their failures toward each other.

The end of the story. They were separated. Loretta spoke of it as a divorce. Perhaps some grounds were found for annulment. Loretta got custody of the child and has continued to work and to support him. She has continued to live near her family. Recently, she has begun to get a very "blooming" look. When this was pointed out to her, she grinned all over her face, like a romantic adolescent. She said, "I have a new boy friend." When prodded, she went on. Well—he was just everything that her husband had not been. To quote: "He is a nice, steady Italian man (by which she meant a man with Italian parents). He thinks that everything I do is just right. He loves my family and my boy. And . . . he thinks I am a wonderful cook!"

Suppose, now, in addition to these differences growing out of their respective national origins, George and Loretta had been Roman Catholic and Methodist, respectively. It is easy to see how all the problems growing out of their religious faiths would have been intensified and complicated by their different national origins.

SOCIAL-CLASS DIFFERENCES IN INTERFAITH MARRIAGES

Finally, there is a social-class aspect to many interfaith marriages. To prevent any possible misunderstanding, we hasten to add at once that the phrase *social class* is used here, not as a term of social snobbery, or to imply distinctions of innate worth between people, but to indicate that people live at different levels and in ways that differ from each other. Thus a corporation lawyer or an investment broker lives differently from the elevator operator in his building.

A considerable number of marriages in this country are between people who have been reared at different class levels. This is because ours is an open-class system, in which social "terraces" have been less sharply defined and maintained than in other and older countries, because of our democratic traditions, and because of the emphasis upon personal choice in the selection of mates.

We are concerned here with these marriages because a certain number of interfaith marriages are also interclass marriages. Perhaps the chief reason for this is that the religious denominations of a community often differ in the social prestige or status attributed to them. Thus one church will be referred to as the place where the "upper crust" goes to worship; another church will be attended largely by people living on the "wrong side of the railroad tracks"; and still others will rate in between.

Among Protestant groups in this country, denominations tend to be socially evaluated, often quite clearly. Some sly wag has pointed this out about the Protestant churches in the South in this way: When you are barefooted, you go

to the Baptist church; when you buy shoes, you join the
Methodist church; when you buy store clothes, you go to
the Presbyterian church; and when you buy store liquor,
then you are an Episcopalian.

In more serious vein, we cite Professor W. Lloyd War-
ner, who has spent much time studying the social-class
structure in this country. He says that Episcopalians and
Unitarians generally rank higher in the social scale than do
Methodists and Baptists, with Congregationalists and Presbyterians somewhere in between. As to the Roman Catholic
membership, Father Thomas, a Catholic sociologist, points
out that, because of the ethnic origin of so many of its members, their social status is mostly lower and middle class.

Over against these generalizations, there are many outstanding regional differences in the social status of most
churches. There are areas in the South, and no doubt else-
where, where the Methodist Episcopal church ranks as high
as the Episcopalian; there are communities where the "blue-
stocking Presbyterians" are "top drawer"; there are Catholic parishes which rate socially with the best; and there often
are wide social-status differences between old, established
German Jewish congregations and the more recently arrived
Russian Jews. Much of this social rating of denominations
and of separate churches grows out of the ethnic makeup of
the group, the relative time of their arrival in this country,
and the extent to which they have become established.

All of this is highly important in the study of marriage
and the family. Marriage is, for many persons—more often
for women than for men, perhaps—a status-achieving device. There is the frequent calculated interest in "marrying
up." In a recent nationwide study in which the senior author
played a part, a great many mixed marriages were of this
kind. Usually women, members of the church with the

lower social prestige, married men who were members of a church with higher social standing. In these cases, therefore, the interfaith marriage combined two persons not only of two different religious cultures but also of two different social backgrounds. ;

EACH INTERFAITH MARRIAGE IS UNIQUE

Thus far, the more general aspects of interfaith marriages have been pointed out. The differences between religious groups are fundamental and pervasive. They include differences in religious convictions, and these are not unimportant. But they include much more. Behind the beliefs are differences in behavior, in observances in the daily life, in attitudes, in values, and in moral judgments. Reinforcing these often are the cultural survivals of different national origin groups, going back to the lives of their forebears in the country of their origin. In still other cases there are differences in social prestige between the persons making an interfaith marriage, thus adding another dimension to the resulting problems.

There is, however, an individual aspect to all of this. Much depends upon the attitudes of the persons marrying toward religion and the church. How conscious are they of religion, and its importance in life? How devoted are they to their respective churches? What have been their attitudes toward religions other than their own? How introspective are they, given to analyzing and philosophizing about their ways of living and thinking? These questions are vital, because each partner to an interfaith marriage will approach the problems of such a marriage on the basis of his or her answers to these questions.

It is obvious, then, that each interfaith marriage is unique,

differing in some respects from every other one. Each represents its own distinctive combination of cultural values, traditional attachments, and prestige position of two persons.
Each represents the union of the ways in which the matrimonial mates refract their religious backgrounds. Finally,
each interfaith marriage is unique because every marriage,
regardless of religious factors, is unique. For every marriage brings together two different persons, each with his
own distinctive array of personal traits and characteristics.

And people can differ in many respects. The number and
variety of traits which students of personality have emphasized are amazing. They include physical traits, such as phy-
sique, physiognomy, and physical efficiency; intelligence
traits, such as learning ability, imagination, memory, judgment, and intuition; aptitudes of varying kinds and degrees;
temperamental qualities, such as activity, drive, tenacity,
mood, and emotional level; a host of attitudes, including
spontaneity and negativism, sympathy and antagonism,
candor and evasiveness, self-assurance and timidity, domination and submissiveness, sociability and self-seeking, and
many others; and patterns of life organization, working
habits, manners, ethical code, esthetic code, social type, and
philosophy of life. All of these in turn combine to form
introverted, extroverted, neurotic or psychopathic types.
Small wonder that many students of marriage and family
life have confined their efforts to these personal rather than
to the broader cultural factors.

Perhaps this is the place then for us to emphasize that the
factors which combine to create a happy or an unhappy
marriage are manifold. The life of every family is very complex, so complex that Quintilian, the famous Roman rheto-
rician, once remarked that for "exploring human nature,
one household is large enough." Obviously, then, in empha-

sizing the real nature of interfaith marriages, we do not mean in any way to emphasize interfaith harmony as *the* key to successful marriages, or interfaith differences as *the* explanation of their failure. All life, and this includes married life, is so complex that to offer single explanations for its problems is both misleading and naive.

To summarize, then, we have sought in this particular part of our discussion to point out the real meaning of interfaith marriages, that they involve the union of two differing ways of living and thinking in life's most intimate relationship; that these differences are very pervasive, and are particularly manifest in patterns of sexual behavior; and that national origin and social-class differences sharpen and reinforce these religious differences; and finally how, within these cultural factors, each interfaith marriage is unique because it unites two distinctive personalities.

CHAPTER FOUR

Who, Where, and Why

How prevalent are mixed marriages in the United States? Are they increasing or decreasing? What are the reasons for the change? Why are these facts important? What about the larger social situation of marriage and mate selection which bears upon the problem of mixed marriages? These are questions which inevitably present themselves to anyone who is concerned, either as participant or student of the problem, and the attempt to answer them constitutes the substance of this chapter.

There are three main reasons why certain basic facts in the mathematics of mixed marriages are important. First, they tell us the dimensions of the problem. Do mixed marriages occur so rarely that we may dismiss them as scattered incidents in the human drama of a large and populous country? Or are they so commonplace as to suggest that they are a part of the normal marriage pattern? Or are they a substantial minority of the total number of marriages, small enough to be abnormal but large enough to be serious? To know the dimensions of a problem tells us much about its seriousness and something about its nature.

Secondly, it is important to know in what direction the problem is moving. Just as the doctor wants repeated readings of the temperature of his ailing patient so that he may know how the illness is progressing, so the trend in the facts about mixed marriage has meaning for the intelligent reader.

Finally, it means much, if one has made a mixed marriage or is contemplating one, to know that other persons are occupied with the same questions. In seeking to help their patients, psychiatrists often try to show them that their trials and tribulations are not unique but that they occur in the lives of many persons. This gives perspective, and perspective of one's self and one's problems is always helpful.

THE PREVALENCE OF MIXED MARRIAGES

It is a matter of simple honesty to say, here and now, that no one knows exactly how many mixed marriages occur in the United States in any given period of time. The reason for this is that information concerning religion is not usually asked when application is made for a license to marry. Applicants are asked for many other facts: their age; their residence; their marital status; in some states, for proof of freedom from venereal disease; in other states, for time of divorce, if such has been their experience; and various other items. But only Iowa requires information concerning religious affiliation, and has done so only recently. It was in 1953 that the question of religious denomination was placed on that state's new statistical forms for the reporting of marriages and divorces to the state office. It might be added that our Canadian neighbors to the north have regularly obtained such information on marriage and divorce records, as do various European and South American countries. Its lack on a nationwide scale in this country is a serious omission in our marriage data, and can perhaps only be explained as a "leaning over backward" in our historic policy of religious toleration.

In the absence of complete official counts of mixed marriages, we are driven to the use of available substitutes. These consist of special and restricted studies which, when combined, give us not an exact but a relatively reliable answer.

First, there is fairly satisfactory information on all mixed marriages involving Roman Catholics in which Catholic nuptials are held. These are usually spoken of as valid mixed marriages, meaning that, although one of the marital partners is non-Catholic, the marriage is performed in compliance with the requirements laid down by the church and sanctioned by it. Such valid mixed marriages are listed year by year with reasonable accuracy in *The Official Catholic Directory*.

Father John L. Thomas, a Catholic sociologist at St. Louis University, has examined these data for recent years, and concludes that during the last two decades mixed marriages account for from one-fourth to one-third of all valid Catholic marriages. To this proportion must be added those mixed marriages which the Catholic church terms invalid, because they are not performed in accordance with the requirements of the church. Accurate information on this point is lacking, but Catholic studies show that each year between 15 and 25 per cent of all marriages involving Catholics are invalid. Combining these two sets of figures, derived from Catholic sources, it is conservative to say that today, each year, at least one-half of all Catholics marrying find their mates outside of the Roman Catholic church. It is pertinent to add here that about one-fifth of the nation's population is affiliated with the Catholic church, and that presumably one-fifth of the nation's marriages would involve affiliated Catholics.

A second source of information on a comprehensive scale is to be found in a nationwide study of marriages of members of the United Lutheran Church in America. This study, in which the senior author of this volume participated, secured information for 382 Lutheran congregations, scattered throughout twenty-eight states, the District of Columbia, five provinces in Canada, and the Virgin Islands. It showed that, for the five-year period 1946-50, of the Lutherans in these congregations who married, 58 per cent found their mates outside of the Lutheran church. Of all the Lutherans who married outside their church, one out of five (20.5 per cent) married Roman Catholics; close to another one-fifth (18.8 per cent) married nonchurch members; and almost three-fifths married members of other Protestant churches. The percentage that married Jews and other non-Protestants was very small.

Finally, reference might be made to the record in Iowa where, since 1953, information on the religious denomination of those marrying is required. These figures tend to show that interfaith marriages are even more numerous than is generally recognized, especially for Catholics.

If these studies are representative of the present situation in the United States, and it is believed that they are, it is safe to conclude that about one-half of all church members who marry find their mates outside their respective churches.

VARIATIONS IN THE PROPORTION OF MIXED MARRIAGES

Because a particular reader may find that this over-all summary is different from the facts in his own church or community, it is well to point out that the mathematics of mixed marriages vary a good deal from place to place.

First, there are the differences from one city or region to another. Father Thomas, the eminent Catholic sociologist, shows that the mixed-marriage rates for Catholics in such dioceses as Raleigh, North Carolina, Charleston, South Carolina, and Nashville, Tennessee, are from four to nine times higher than those in Providence, Rhode Island, Fall River, Massachusetts, and Santa Fe, New Mexico.

Second, there are the variations on the basis of sex. In certain groups women contract more mixed marriages than do the men in those groups. For example, Roman Catholic figures show there are sixty women making mixed marriages for every forty men making such marriages. In the Lutheran study previously referred to, almost twice as many women as men married outside of their church. These sex variations are part in turn of a larger story of mate selection. Various studies show that, while like tends to marry like, whenever lines of education, social class, economic status, race, or national origin are crossed, women in selected groups cross them more frequently than do men in these groups.

It is interesting, too, and quite important, that women tend to cross those lines in an upward rather than a downward direction. As pointed out in the preceding chapter, a mixed marriage seems to be a way by which women achieve a higher status. The Lutheran study of mixed marriages made this particularly clear. In the course of this investigation, information was secured on the relative status of the Lutheran church in the community, as well as the percentage of members by sex who married outside of the church. From these facts it was clear that the lower the status of the Lutheran church the higher the percentages of members marrying outside of the church, with a relatively large proportion of them being women who married in an upward direction.

The prevalence of mixed marriages varies from one faith to another. The rate of Jewish intermarriage as a whole is relatively low in the United States, being opposed by the overwhelming proportion of the Jewish community. Within the Jewish group, significant differences, however, are found. Orthodox Jews, because of their adherence to traditional teachings, make few mixed marriages. Reformed Jews, while more liberal in the face of changing conditions, retain their opposition. Only among agnostic Jews has there been some recent tendency in this direction. Intermarriage between Jews and Catholics is relatively rare. For Catholics, such marriages require "dispensation for disparity of cult," which is rarely given.

THE CHANGING PROPORTION OF MIXED MARRIAGES

Are interfaith marriages increasing, decreasing, or remaining stationary? Here again we must rely on scattered bits of evidence, but all that is obtainable shows quite clearly that they are on the increase.

Father Thomas, after examining the Roman Catholic statistics, concludes that there has been a steady but gradual increase since 1910. The two periods of World War I and World War II showed a considerable increase, in some dioceses as high as 10 per cent. Father Thomas then goes on to predict that there are excellent reasons for thinking that there will be a gradual and steady increase of marriages between Catholics and non-Catholics in the future.

Our other source of information is the study made of Lutherans who made mixed marriages. This covered a fifteen-year period from 1936 to 1950. Grouped by five-year periods, the percentages of Lutherans marrying outside of their church are 46 per cent in 1936-40; 47 per cent in 1941-45; and 58 per cent in 1946-50.

Factors Determining the Rate of Mixed Marriages

Our summary on the mathematics of mixed marriages would not be complete without some reference to the factors which seem to influence their number. An understanding of these factors will not only explain why the percentages of such marriages vary from one place to another, but also, on the basis of these factors, what we may reasonably expect in the years ahead.

To begin with, a great deal depends on the religious makeup of the population in any particular area, and the relative number of persons of marriageable age in any religious group. We are tempted to make a generalization here and say that the smaller the number of unmarried persons of marriageable age in any religious group the higher will be the percentage of persons in that group who make mixed marriages. Certainly that is what many of our statistics show, and the explanation is a quite obvious one. When single persons of marriageable age live in areas where there are many other single persons of the opposite sex who go to the same church and/or who live nearby, they will find their mates among them; when such persons are not available, they turn to other groups. Consider, for example, some of the Catholic data on mixed (valid) marriages. In selected dioceses where the Catholic population is 2 per cent or less of the total, the percentages of mixed marriages range from sixty to seventy; where Catholics constitute one-half or more of the total population, the percentages fall below twenty, and in some cases below ten.

In many places a second population factor operates to reinforce the above. This is the national origin of the various elements in the population and their religious persuasions. In some of these national origin groups there is a strong "we-feeling," with a corresponding reluctance to marry outside of the group, regardless of religious differences. Thus, for example, among Germans the sense of a common German origin may tend to unite Catholics and Protestants in a common bond, and result in a higher percentage of mixed marriages than would ordinarily occur. On the other hand, a relatively large German community, mostly of Lutheran persuasion, living in close proximity to an Italian Catholic area, may confine its marriages rather strictly within the German community, with the result that the percentage of mixed marriages would be rather low.

One more population factor must be noted. People today are much more mobile than formerly. Especially is this true of our younger people. And increased mobility means more contacts with people of all kinds—of different religions as well as other social circumstances. Modern methods of transportation have much to do with this, as have present-day emphases upon higher education and the lure of employment opportunities. The automobile and the airplane have revolutionized the recreational habits and travel opportunities of peoples of all ages, and romance flourishes on recreational contacts. Finally, there are the requirements of military service which uproot most of our young men and transplant them to new areas with social contacts of many different sorts. Influences of this kind not only expose young people to new contacts but they also tend to weaken the hold of old group controls.

CHANGING METHODS OF MATE SELECTION

Mixed marriages are one aspect of the larger area of mate selection, and one can understand them better in the light of recent trends in that larger area.

1. One of these trends concerns the age of marriage. Most people believe, perhaps because of the large increase in the number of young people in college, that they marry later and later in life. Exactly the opposite is true. Back in 1890, when life began theoretically so much earlier for the young, the average man married shortly after he turned twenty-six. Today he marries at twenty-two. The average young woman in 1890 married at twenty-two; today she marries at twenty.

Another indication of what is happening can be seen from comparisons in specific age groups. According to the most recent United States census returns, the proportion of men at ages twenty to twenty-four years who are married almost doubled during the fifteen-year period from 1940 to 1955. The change in percentage married was from 27 per cent in 1940 to 51 per cent in 1955. For women in the same age period and during the same fifteen-year period, the proportion married increased from 51 per cent in 1940 to 69 per cent in 1955. Even more striking are the changes for the age group fifteen to nineteen years old. For boys, the percentage increased from 1.7 per cent to 3.3 per cent; for girls, from 11 to 17 per cent.

In no other country of the Western world do people marry so young. In the age bracket from twenty to twenty-four, the United States had twice as many married men and 50 per cent more married women than will be found proportionately in England and Wales. In comparison to Ireland, we have nine times as many married men in that age bracket and four times as many married women. The only European country that comes at all close to our record—and not very close, at that—is Yugoslavia. Whatever the reasons for this may be, and there are many, there is in this country today an almost compulsive drive to marry at the earliest possible moment. Not only do many parents, in an undue haste to step out from under their responsibilities as parents, encourage this, but the impersonalized life of the large community creates a feeling that it is best to grasp the first opportunity since it also may be the last.

This low age of marriage must be coupled with our lengthening period of formal education. Taken together, these two facts mean that an increasing number of young people move from the sheltered life of the schoolroom to the stark realities of a job, a wife or husband, and a child, with little or no intervening experience. It is a big transition for many young people, on many fronts, and in a very short period of time.

2. Modern methods do not always make for wise choice of lifelong matrimonial partners. The current emphases often are upon success in party-giving, dancing, sports, petting, and the skilful manipulation of a patois that in our day was called a "good line." There tends to be an impersonality about present-day courtship such as one finds in other aspects of social life. We go to a cocktail party or reception of some sort, observe all the niceties, say the acceptable, innocuous things, and, by skilfully avoiding any controversial subject, create the impression of being "nice," "adjustable," and having a "pleasing personality." All this, in courtship as in more mature social life, involves a kind of social maneuvering, little of which touches upon or reveals those things which are vital for living together in life's most intimate relationship for the next forty or more years.

Many young people tend to choose their matrimonial partners in the same way they buy a car—without ever looking under the hood. Both car and mate must be streamlined. Not that this whole problem of selection is ignored in our current books and teaching. Rather is it stressed to the point of overemphasis. But what are extolled are superficial qualities of a romantic kind, instead of cultural values which have meaning for human living together. When one thinks in terms of a lifelong union, being a good mixer and having a presentable pair of legs are less important than what one thinks about God, the family meal, and a crying baby. Obviously, all this bears directly on the subject of interfaith marriages, because differences of this sort are exactly the kind which superficial methods of mate selection will consider but lightly, if at all. Religious differences between a boy and a girl seem very trivial at a school dance, a wienerroast, or a cocktail party, but they become the core of father-mother relationships after the birth of the first child.

3. Intensifying all this is the fact that modern youth claims the full prerogative of making its own mistakes. In the field of marriage this means that parents and kinsfolk are not to interfere in the process of mate selection. Perhaps there is value in this emphasis, but parental selection of mates has the support of many centuries in the experience of all the historic civilizations. Modern youth does not always know better than the verdict of forty centuries. There is at least something to be said for the old Chinese custom whereby, in the preliminary stages, the families of the young couple met with each other, entertained each other, and gave gifts to each other. Coupled with this was the very helpful facesaving custom of employing the astrologer to cast the future for the courting couple. Happily, his forecast could always be modified or rationalized to support the judgment of the

elders. When one thinks in terms of an intended lifelong union, this old custom stands in odd contrast to the modern circumstance in which the parents of the marrying pair meet for the first time at the ceremony, if at all. And, as a pertinent aside, who is caught "holding the bag" when daughter Mary brings home to her parents the two young products of her big mistake? Thousands of parents know the answer to this one.

Some Current Conceptions of Marriage

The number, the nature, and the changing proportion of mixed marriages must also be considered against the background of some current conceptions of marriage. Five of these are quite apparent and are much emphasized today. We shall consider each in turn.

1. The first of these, and foremost in certain respects, has been the change in the conception of the nature and control of marriage. Time was, and it remained so for centuries, when marriage was under the exclusive control of the church. Not only was the marriage ceremony solely a religious rite, but the church dictated the conditions under which the marriage might occur and, in certain rare cases, be terminated. The Roman Catholic conception of marriage as a sacrament, still maintained, is an example of such a conception of marriage.

We Americans live in a country where marriage is recognized as a civil contract, authorized by the state, viewed as a legal contract between two persons, and capable of being dissolved by the same authority. True, many marriages are still solemnized in churches by clergymen acting as agents of the state, but this religious touch adds nothing to the legality of the contract.

Behind this shift has been the slowly declining influence of the church in the control of marriage per se, of the marriage of its members, and the details related to their family life.

2. Supporting this change has been the increasing secularization of our Western life and thought, to which reference has been made earlier in this volume. A secular society is one in which resistance to change is at a minimum; it is rational and open-minded to a point often of indifference to the old and the sacred. It is a society in which a wide choice of conduct is permitted to the individual, including his marriage. Secularization combines many elements—the spread of science, increasing material well-being, the diffusion of education, and the encouragement of the critical faculty. Similarly, its influences ramify into many directions. The rejection of older, traditional ideas about mate selection and marriage certainly is one of these. The lessened control by the church over the behavior of its members, including their marriage, is another.

One can see this latter influence of secularization quite clearly, among others, in the case of such a distinctive religious group as the Jews. For centuries their survival as an ethnic and religious group has been due to the isolating aspects of their behavior, as dictated by their religious leaders. This included not only their abstinence from marriage with other groups but also the maintenance of many rituals in the family and other aspects of their daily lives. With the decline of these rituals, and with increased opportunities for social contacts, marriages between Jews and Gentiles have increased.

3. One of the most distinctive current emphases regarding marriage is the high premium set upon romantic attraction. As presently interpreted, this means that you marry solely

for love, that marriage is the final realization of romantic attraction. One might call this the Hollywood conception of marriage, for the movies have done much to foster the lushness of its appeal. Moreover, the 1,968 professors who were reported in a survey several years ago as giving 657 courses in marriage and family problems in 550 colleges and universities have fallen into full step with the movies, at least if the books which they use in their courses may be taken as a criterion.

But the critical reader will say: there is nothing new or unusual or alarming about love. And one must agree completely. Strong emotional attraction between persons of the opposite sex is as old as the human heartbeat. Love is one of the things which makes the world go round, and makes it a brighter place in which to live.

The point that is stressed here is the modern tendency to make love the primary, and often the sole, basis of marriage selection. This is new, and it goes back no farther in human history than the twelfth and thirteenth centuries when the French troubadours first introduced it into the stream of Western living. Previous to this, marriages were invariably arranged on the basis of more practical considerations, such as the judgment of parents and kinsfolk, the exchange of financial agreements, or the promotion of a career. Coinciding with this more prosaic practice, there was usually a long period of courtship during which the prospective mates and their respective families learned to know and test each other's mettle, for what people in other cultures know, and what we so largely ignore today, is that marriage is not only the union of two individuals but also of two cultural backgrounds and the kinship groups which are the personification and source of it.

4. Individualism is a complementary value that is much emphasized as a basis for marriage in contemporary America. The purpose of marriage, according to this conception, is the happiness of the mates and their respective personality development. A good marriage is one that contributes fully and freely to the development and enrichment of the personality of its contractors; a poor marriage is one that hinders it.

This particular emphasis is, of course, but one phase of a much larger ideological pattern as distinctly American as ancestor worship has been characteristic among the Chinese. Many children encounter this pattern early in their school careers, where they are encouraged to express themselves. The stronger this emphasis in a school the more "progressive" it is said to be. Later on, this individualistic trend expresses itself in freedom of choice of mate, often disregarding the advice and admonition of parents, kinsfolk, pastor, priest, rabbi, or any of the traditional values and modes in mate selection. After marriage, this philosophy tends to be maintained. Almost from the beginning, many young couples today organize their lives on an individualistic basis. The employment of married women, so current today, makes this still more inevitable, so that husbands and wives become potential if not actual competitors as wage earners.

It seems proper to point out the logical conclusion of these emphases upon romance and individualism. It is this: when one marries solely or largely for personal happiness and fulfilment, then one must leave the mate for the same reason. If living with Jane Brown is essential to one's fullest personality development in 1953, what happens in 1956 when only Mary Smith can serve this purpose? If personality development, and romance too, is the basis for marriage, then obviously when the basis disappears the marriage is over.

5. Finally, the more one ponders current news and marital behavior, the more one comes to sense a certain air or attitude of experimentation about marriage, as though we were watching exercises in a test tube in a laboratory.

To the admonition and reminders of elders and sages, the current generation answers something like this. Yes, we know about the wisdom of the ages. We know that this and that have been the collective experience of mankind. But let's try this. It may work. Other new things have been tried and have worked. Look at jet planes and penicillin. Besides, if it doesn't work, we can always try it again. Divorce is not too difficult. And it is relatively common now.

In summary, then, we have tried to emphasize that the number of marriages that cross the religious line is large and is increasing relatively; that such marriages do not exist *in vacuo*; that they are part of the whole contemporary scene of courtship, mate selection, and marriage; and as a result are subject to the same factors and influences that operate in the background of all marriages.

CHAPTER FIVE

The Churches and Mixed Marriage

Why do churches concern themselves with mixed marriages? What are the attitudes of the leading churches toward such marriages? Why do they take such attitudes? Are their reasons merely a matter of self-interest? How do they appear to lay students? These are pertinent questions to raise, and this chapter is devoted to a frank discussion of them.

To deal properly with the churches' attitude toward interfaith marriages it is necessary to see the basic problem in its larger perspective. We can do this if we remind ourselves that every group with any sense of unity concerns itself with the behavior of its members. The higher the degree of group cohesion and consciousness the greater is the concern with such behavior. Certain aspects of this behavior will receive special attention, such as the relationships between members of the group and nonmembers, the admission and recruiting of new members, and the withdrawal of old members. The reason these receive particular emphasis is that they involve the life and continuance of the group.

Examples of this can be found at every hand. Two thousand years ago, tribal societies laid down the strictest requirements whereby one could be born or adopted into the tribe, or live in it. Student fraternities and sororities exercise many controls over their members, particularly those involving admission or withdrawal. Perhaps no more flagrant example could be found than in the practices and policies of labor organizations. Or, there are the gangs of adolescents who pounce upon boys from the "outside" coming to court girls in "their" neighborhoods. There is obviously nothing new or unusual in the principle involved in all of these cases, nor in its application by church groups. All of the established religions have sought to control to some extent the marriage and reproductive behavior of their members through the centuries of their existence.

THE ATTITUDE OF JUDAISM

From the beginning, Jews have looked with disfavor upon intermarriage with non-Jews, and for centuries their survival as a distinct religious and ethnic group has been due in large measure to their abstinence from marriage with other groups. The language of Deuteronomy (7:1-4) is direct and clear: "When the Lord thy God shall bring thee into the Land whither thou goest to possess it, and hath cast out many nations before thee . . . thou shalt make no covenant with them . . . Neither shalt thou make marriages with them; thy daughter thou shalt not give unto his son, nor his daughter shalt thou take unto thy son. For they will turn away thy son from following me, that they may serve other gods: so will the anger of the Lord be kindled against you, and destroy thee suddenly."

Later, after their return from the Babylonian captivity, the prophets Ezra and Nehemiah insisted with great vigor that the strange wives that had been acquired be put away, even though there were children by them, and priests were among the guilty ones. In his confession of the national sins, Ezra says: "For they have taken of their daughters for themselves, and for their sons: so that the holy seed have mingled themselves with the people of *those* lands: yea, the hand of the princes and rulers hath been chief in this trespass. And when I heard this thing, I rent my garment and my mantle, and plucked off the hair of my head and of my beard, and sat down astonied" (Ezra 9:2, 3). In like vein, Nehemiah, in organizing the services of the Levites against the national sins, made it a matter of first resolve "that we would not give our daughters unto the people of the land, nor take their daughters for our sons." (Nehemiah 10:30. *See also* 13:23-25.)

The passages which have been quoted established the policies laid down by rabbinical authorities in post-biblical times. Marriage with Gentiles was forbidden, but permission was granted if the Gentiles were converted to Judaism. Punishment for violation of this ban was known as "cherem," and was equivalent to excommunication. This became the established procedure both in the law of the Talmud and the rabbinical code.

The Jews brought with them to this country their ancient opposition. In keeping with their status as a minority group, this has taken the form of recognizing the validity of such marriages but opposing them as a threat to the survival of Judaism. For many years, however, rabbis who followed the German Reformed movement were somewhat lenient in matters of this kind, as against the more stringent attitude of Orthodox and Conservative rabbis. Then, in 1909, the Central Conference of American Rabbis, a group of Reformed Jewish clergymen, passed a resolution that declared "that mixed marriages are contrary to the tradition of the Jewish religion and should therefore be discouraged by the American rabbinate." Twenty-eight years later, in 1937, a survey showed that 67 per cent of the Reformed rabbis would not officiate at religious intermarriages, and 21 per cent did so only if the couple promised to bring up their children as Jews or that the couple would join a Jewish congregation, or both.

Two other indications of a trend toward a more conservative attitude among Reformed Jewish clergymen can be cited. One is the treatment of the subject in a textbook published in 1941 for Jewish young people attending the Reformed Sunday school. In it, reference is made to the fact that Jewish-Gentile romances often end in tragic circumstances, that the majority of Gentile college students are opposed to intermarriage with Jews, and that Jews who intermarry usually are lost to Judaism. No advantages or benefits in such marriages are mentioned. The other indication was the reaffirmation, in 1947, by the Central Conference of its 1909 declaration, with additional stipulations calling for religious ceremonies to follow civil mixed marriages and the religious education and confirmation of children born to such marriages.

These regulatory measures are a fair representation of the attitude of Jewish leaders, held with basic consistency for several thousand years. Rabbis and Jewish lay writers have agreed upon the difficulties that inhere in such marriages, pointing out their dangers to marital happiness and to the survival of Jews as a distinct religious group. Wherever Jews have intermarried freely, Jewish writers like Maurice Fishberg pointed out some years ago, they lose their identity as a people.

THE MOHAMMEDAN POLICY

The Mohammedan law of marriage ordains that the confession of Islam by the husband is one of the conditions for all marriages. A Moslem male, however, is allowed to marry a free "scriptural woman" (a Christian or Jewish woman) but not an idolatress, i.e., a non-Christian polytheist. Although the union with such outsiders might be valid, it has been frowned upon and regarded as "abhorrent." Few such possibilities, of course, have been available to the Mohammedan woman, nor is the situation likely to arise since the Mohammedan way of life permits her little or no contact with an "alien" male.

THE EARLY CHRISTIAN POLICY

From its very beginnings, the Christian church has been opposed to unions with persons outside the fold. In his second epistle to the Corinthians (II Corinthians 6:14), St. Paul advises: "Be ye not unequally yoked together with unbelievers: for what fellowship hath righteousness with unrighteousness? and what communion hath light with darkness?" This point of view, reiterated by the early church fathers, such as St. Cyprian and Tertullian, was expressed formally by the Council of Elvira (300-306) which forbade Christian girls to marry "infidels, Jews, heretics or priests of the pagan rites." Emperor Constantine the Great, soon after his conversion to Christianity, prohibited (339) all intermarriages between Christians and Jews, and a subsequent Roman statute of 388 declared such intermarriages to be

adulterous. Later emperors and councils of the church (La-
odicea, 343-81; Hippo, 393; Orléans, 538; Toledo, 589; and
Rome, 743) added the more fully developed injunctions of
church and state.

Not that these injunctions were always obeyed. In the
early days the number of Christians was small, and then, as
now, limited opportunities for marriage within one's own
group led to marriage on the outside. Also, during the period
when the Christian church was struggling for a secure foot-
hold, mixed marriages were often encouraged as a way of
proselyting. There are many references to such marriages
in the literature of this period.

ROMAN CATHOLIC ATTITUDES AND POLICIES

A very large part of the problem of mixed marriages
grows out of marriages between Catholics and non-Catholics. Many of the resultant difficulties grow out of the
definite stand taken by the Catholic church regarding such
marriages. It seems proper therefore to examine somewhat
more fully its views in the matter.

To understand the attitudes and policies of the Roman
Catholic church toward mixed marriages, it is necessary to
see clearly the Catholic conception of the nature and purpose of marriage. Marriage, according to Roman Catholics,
is divine in origin, whatever additional human aspects and
purposes there may be. It is intended by the Creator to per-
petuate the creative act and to beget children of God. Other
ends, such as mutual helpfulness and love, are secondary.

It was St. Augustine, back in the fifth century, who
formulated the classic statement of the three "goods" of
marriage as loyalty, children, and indissoluble unity. This
statement was further clarified by St. Thomas Aquinas, and

was given final form by the Council of Trent (1545-63) in what we shall see is the basic policy of the Roman Catholic church.

Moreover, and this is an important fact, marriage is declared to be a sacrament, similar in nature to baptism, confirmation, the Lord's supper, or extreme unction. As such, it is under the control of the church, which is the divinely appointed custodian of all sacraments. Marriage is a part of the church's jurisdiction because it has the right to apply and interpret the Divine Law. This right is not one of concession or sufferance, received from human or temporal sources, but from Christ himself.

Furthermore, according to the Roman Catholic view, its church is a special restricted society, established by Jesus for the purpose of saving all of mankind. Individuals are admitted to this society by the rite (sacrament) of baptism. As members of this society they are subject to its rules and obligations. Marriage is one of the areas of life in this society. Admittance to it is a matter of choice, but, once chosen, persons entering it are subject to the rules of the society regarding it.

Since marriage is a sacrament, it follows that a marriage between a Catholic and a non-Catholic involves a communion "in sacred things with those outside the fold," and thus degrades the holy character of matrimony. "The very intimacy of the union necessarily established between those joined in wedlock," writes Father Fanning in *The Catholic Encyclopedia*, "requires a concordance above all in their religious sentiments."

From the foregoing, one can clearly see why the Roman Catholic church, throughout its history, has opposed marriages between Catholics and non-Catholics. At first, the opposition was directed against Jews and Mohammedans, but after the Protestant Reformation in the sixteenth century the "new heretics" were added to the list. It was this new group of problems which led the Council of Trent, previously referred to, to declare that all matrimonial unions between Catholics and non-Catholics were null and void unless entered into before the ecclesiastical authority. Since that time the canon law of the church has worked out the details of its control on the basis of experience in many different countries.

It does not seem necessary to go into these details here, nor to refer to the changes and modifications that the church has made in Protestant countries and in the face of the civil control of marriage. Suffice it to summarize the present situation in this country, as shown in the following selected facts which are part of the larger structure of the church's canonical law.

1. The canon law recognizes differences in religious faith as one of the "prohibitory impediments" to marriage.

2. Two kinds of such marriages are recognized. One is between a Catholic and a baptized non-Catholic; the other, between a Catholic and an unbaptized non-Catholic. These two require different kinds of dispensation.

3. When a priest is approached with a request for a dispensation to enter a mixed marriage, three conditions are imposed for the granting of such a request:

    (a) There must be "just and weighty reasons" for such a request, since a Catholic should not expose himself or herself to such grave dangers as inhere in such a marriage, without a proportionately grave reason.

    (b) Certain guarantees must be given by both the Catholic and the non-Catholic parties in writing. The details of these documents vary from one diocese to another, but the essentials are the same everywhere. As an example, two forms are presented here:

ANTE-NUPTIAL CONTRACT AND PROMISES

To be signed in duplicate in the presence of the priest by the parties entering a mixed marriage, and by two witnesses.

To be signed by the Non-Catholic Party

I, the undersigned, not a member of the Catholic Church, wishing to contract marriage with the Catholic party whose signature is also hereinafter affixed to this mutual agreement, being of sound mind and perfectly free, and only after understanding fully the import of my action, do hereby enter into this mutual agreement, understanding that the execution of this agreement and the promises therein contained are made in contemplation of and in consideration for the consent, marriage and consequent change of status of the hereinafter mentioned Catholic party, and I, therefore, hereby agree:

1. That I will not interfere in the least with the free exercise of the Catholic party's religion;

2. That I will adhere to the doctrine of the sacred indissolubility of the marriage bond, so that I cannot contract a second marriage while my consort is still alive, even though a civil divorce may have been obtained;

3. That all the children, both boys and girls, that may be born of this union shall be baptized and educated solely in the faith of the Roman Catholic Church, even in the event of the death of my Catholic consort. In case of dispute, I furthermore, hereby fully agree that the custody of all the children shall be given to such guardians as to assure the faithful execution of this covenant and promise;

4. That I will lead a married life in conformity with the Law of God and the teaching of the Catholic Church regarding birth control, realizing fully the attitude of the Catholic Church in this regard;

5. That no other marriage ceremony shall take place before or after this ceremony by the Catholic priest.

In testimony of which agreement, I do hereby solemnly swear that I will observe the above agreement and faithfully execute the promises therein contained, and do now affix my signature in approval thereof.

Then there follows a space for the signature of the non-Catholic party after which the four promises to be made by the Catholic party are listed, preceded by a preliminary statement similar to that given above. The Catholic promises:

1. That I shall have all my children, both boys and girls, that may be born of this union, baptized and educated solely in the faith of the Roman Catholic Church. I understand that in case of my death or in the event of a dispute, the custody of all the children shall be given to such guardians as to assure the faithful execution of this covenant and promise;

2. That I will practice my Catholic religion faithfully and will strive, especially by example, prayer and the frequentation of the Sacraments, to bring about the conversion of my consort;

3. That I will lead a married life in conformity with the Law of God and the teaching of the Catholic Church regarding birth control, realizing fully the attitude of the Catholic Church in this regard;

4. That no other marriage ceremony shall take place before or after this ceremony by the Catholic priest.

(c) There must be "moral certainty that the guarantees will be fulfilled." Perfect certainty is an impossibility, but there must be probable certainty that such promises will be kept. The key questions here are the character of the non-Catholic party and the firmness in the faith of the Catholic party.

4. Marriages for which dispensations are granted must be contracted before a properly accredited priest and at least two witnesses.

5. Mixed marriages made in accordance with these requirements are valid; others are termed invalid.

6. Additional requirements are found in specific dioceses. One example is that the non-Catholic take at least six instructions in Catholic doctrine and the duties of married life. Another is the instruction of the Catholic party in details of procedure.

SELECTED PROTESTANT ATTITUDES AND POLICIES

American Protestantism on the whole had no definite policy toward mixed marriages or formal system for their control for many years. There were various reasons for this, chief among them being the American tradition of civil control of marriage and the Protestant emphasis upon the role of the individual conscience. On the other hand, many Protestant clergymen as individuals opposed them. In recent years this opposition has been crystallizing in formal declarations of attitude, if not in systems of ecclesiastical control. Selected illustrations will follow.

1. *The Presbyterian church.* This church early gave voice to its collective opposition, as the following quotation from one of its publications will show.

The Church also requires that her sons and daughters "marry in the Lord." This phrase, so unfamiliar to modern young adults, has an ancient and honorable usage in the Reformed faith. The *Constitution* of the Presbyterian Church, U.S.A., historically has defined the term by pointing out that all who "profess the true reformed religion" should avoid marriage "with infidels, Papists, or other idolaters." To this grouping are appended also those who are "notoriously wicked" and such as "maintain damnable heresies."

While the wording of the definition reflects the earlier day in which it was formulated, it remains a basis on which the Church continues to educate members to marry within the Protestant Christian fold. With some frequency this stand is reiterated. The General Assembly of 1950, for instance, adopted a resolution reaffirming their firm stand on the issue of marriage with Roman Catholics. To better demonstrate the broadly Protestant nature of the issue, the Assembly purposely adopted the same wording that had been used by the Protestant Episcopal Church the previous year in their General Convention. They resolved earnestly to warn their members

against contracting marriages with Roman Catholics under

the conditions imposed by modern Roman Catholic canon law, especially as these conditions invoke a promise to have their children brought up in a religious system which they cannot themselves accept; and further, because the religious education and spiritual training of their children by word or example is a paramount duty of parents and should never be neglected or left entirely to others, we assert that in no circumstance should a member of this Church give any understanding, as a condition of marriage, that the children should be brought up in the practice of another Communion.

2. *The Methodist church.* This term now unites what was formerly the Methodist Episcopal church, the Methodist Episcopal church South, and the Methodist Protestant church.

Although most leaders of the Methodist church believed that interfaith marriages ought to be discouraged because of the additional stresses and strains upon family life which they involved, it was not until April, 1956, that the Methodist church as such made any official statement regarding such marriages. In a resolution of the General Conference on "The Christian Family," the section on mixed marriages reads as follows:

> Religious convictions should be a strong tie in marriage. Recent research has emphasized the importance of common cultural and religious backgrounds as the foundation for successful marriage. It is therefore strongly urged that each young person consider carefully before becoming engaged to anyone who does not have a similar religious background. It is important that Protestant youth discuss this problem with their ministers before it is too late. Ministers are urged to discuss with both youth and parents the likelihood of failure in mixed marriages.

3. *The United Lutheran Church in America.* Through its Board of Social Missions, the United Lutheran church has attempted for a number of years, to focus the attention of the church more closely on the general problems of marriage and family living, seeking to help congregations build

programs around its published literature. In 1950, the Ministerium of Pennsylvania, a constituent synod, memorialized the United Church "to formulate a church policy and pastoral procedures with reference to the problem of mixed marriages." It was in keeping with these developments that that church's study of mixed marriage, previously referred to, was made.

One feature of that study is of special interest in this connection. This concerns the policies recommended by almost four hundred Lutheran pastors. Of the total number, 17 per cent favored refusal to perform the ceremony, in most cases if the marriage was to a Catholic or Jew; 6 per cent would excommunicate members if the ceremony were performed outside of the Lutheran church; 18 per cent would require both parties to join one church before marriage; 19 per cent would require guarantees that the children be reared as Lutherans in the event of marriages particularly to Catholics and Jews; the remainder either assumed no official position or considered the issue a private matter. A total of 86 per cent, however, favored an extension of educational and counseling services to the congregations in such matters.

A preliminary statement, adopted in 1954 by the Commission of Marriage and Divorce, is now awaiting final action. It includes the following statements:

> The increase of marriages between people of different religious faiths constitutes a special problem. The adjustments necessary in any marriage are, of course, made more difficult if major differences in economic, educational, and cultural levels are in the background of the marriage partners. These differences also affect the acceptance of the marriage by in-laws and friends. . . . Of major concern here is the significance of religious differences in marriage. . . .
> The Church should give increased attention to education and counseling about mixed marriages. Young people should be led to face the issues involved and helped to see that true love of an-

other person should persuade one to desire the other's spiritual
welfare and to wait for marriage until religious unity is assured.

4. *The Protestant Episcopal church.* In 1949, the General
Convention of this church unanimously adopted the follow-
ing resolution, which is similar to one adopted by a previous
Lambeth Conference.

> Resolved, that this convention earnestly warns members of our
> Church against contracting marriages with Roman Catholics un-
> der conditions imposed by modern Roman Catholic canon law,
> especially as these conditions involve a promise to have their
> children brought up under a religious system which they cannot
> themselves accept; and further, because the religious education
> and spiritual training of their children by word and example is
> a paramount duty of parents and should never be neglected nor
> left entirely to others, we assert that in no circumstances should
> a member of this Church give any understanding as a condition
> of marriage, that the children should be brought up in the prac-
> tice of another communion.

5. *The Northern Baptist church.* The following resolution, passed at its Boston Convention in May, 1950, speaks
for itself:

> Whereas, the Roman Catholic Church has published a direc-
> tive to its priests, church members and the general public imply-
> ing that non-Catholic marriages lack the authenticity furnished
> by Roman Catholic ceremonies through instituting disparaging
> restrictions and exceptions; and
> Whereas, the publication of these discriminations affects so
> many young people who unite in marriage in the freedom of our
> American customs and indicates to them that non-Catholic mar-
> riages are of an inferior and less religious nature; therefore, be it
> *Resolved,* that the Northern Baptist Convention repudiate the
> Roman Catholic claim to authoritarianism in marriage and de-
> clare it an invasion of the principles of religious and social free-
> dom. Furthermore, be it
> *Resolved,* that Baptist pastors be urged to inform their young
> people of the menace to their freedom of the imposed authori-
> tarianism of the Roman Catholic Church, not merely in the per-
> formance of marriage but also in the dictated rules regarding the

raising of offspring of mixed marriages in the Roman Catholic Church; and that young people contemplating an interfaith marriage be instructed by their pastors regarding their civil and religious rights under our Baptist standards of religious liberty.

6. *The Southern Baptist church.* In 1951, this church, through its national convention, made a particularly vigorous statement regarding mixed marriages, especially with Roman Catholics. A part of that statement reads as follows:

> The Roman Catholic church assumes an unwarranted and unholy authority when she attempts to control the marriage laws of the state or to ignore or supplant them. The New Testament nowhere teaches that a marriage must be contracted before a priest or minister in order to be valid.
>
> We should teach our Baptist children that marriage is the supreme partnership of life and that it is a violation of the principle of religious liberty to make the promises demanded by the Roman Catholic church. Our children should know the dangers of these promises so that they can take their stand as free, independent American citizens and refuse to make any promises that the Roman Catholic lover does not make. Marriage should not be a one-sided partnership where one gives up everything. It should be equal for both.

7. *The Disciples of Christ.* The following resolution was approved by the International Convention of Disciples of Christ at Oklahoma City in 1950:

> Whereas, Mutual religious convictions, a common philosophy of life, and a similarity of cultural backgrounds are factors which contribute to a happy marriage; and
>
> Whereas, Mutual respect for and sincere tolerance of differences on the part of both persons entering the union are indispensable, so that marriage can be a union of equals; and
>
> Whereas, Some religious bodies (notably the Roman Catholic church) officially forbid their adherents to enter marriage with non-adherents except on the condition that non-adherents subscribe to certain agreements, particularly that the children of such a union be trained in the faith of the adherent, which in effect destroys any basis for tolerance and equality;
>
> Whereas, Failure to understand and adequately to appreciate

the implications of such agreements, before mutual attachment makes objective evaluation impossible, frequently leads later to disillusionment, family conflict and heartbreak;

Therefore, Be It *Resolved*, That this international Convention of Disciples of Christ urge parents, ministers and leaders of young people to provide in the home, in the church and through the normal channels of the teaching program instruction that will help youth, before or as they arrive at the age of forming intimate friendships between the sexes, to understand and appreciate the divergent interpretations relative to marriage held by different religious bodies; and further

Be It *Resolved*, That we request our young people to seek an understanding of the principles which underlie their Christian faith, to give prayerful consideration when faced with a situation where their wedding vows would entail agreements disparaging their basic Christian beliefs; and further

Be It *Resolved*, That we urge our young people to stand on their rights as self-respecting Christians, and that in no event they enter into a marriage contract which places them in a position of disadvantage in their family relationship and in the training of their children.

8. *Other Protestant Expressions.*

Recently, the Commission on Christian Social Action of the Evangelical and Reformed church, at the direction of the general synod of that church, has been studying the subject of interfaith marriages. Several small Protestant sects excommunicate members who marry outside of their particular churches. Finally, mention should be made of the attitude of the Federal Council of Churches of Christ, as expressed in the declaration of its Committee on Marriage and the Home. This reads in part as follows: "Where intolerable conditions are imposed . . . persons contemplating a mixed marriage should be advised not to enter it."

> Religion is a basic interest in human life, and differences in religion, if these are fundamental, may strain a marriage to the point of breaking, especially where they are aggravated by ecclesiastical interference.
>
> No religious body which confesses itself Christian can tolerate

the imposition upon one of its own members of the requirements of another religious body by which the religious scruples of that member are aroused, or action repugnant to reason and conscience is forced upon him by an authority which he does not acknowledge.

For example, if one of the partners to a mixed marriage submits to the dictation of such an authority and promises that his children will be brought up in a faith which he does not share, reason and conscience are offended, the seeds of future discord are sowed at the very outset of married life, and the prospect of true marriage, with conjunction of mind and soul, becomes remote.

Or if either partner enters upon the union as a propagandist, determined through the intimacies of marriage to subvert the religious faith of the other, disaster is imminent.

REASONS FOR CHURCH OPPOSITION

It seems clear that opposition to mixed marriages is not confined to any one faith but is a general policy of all churches, differing only in degree and details. When we try to understand the reasons for this, four are very evident.

1. Mixed marriages are a threat to membership strength, constituting a problem of church leakage. Various writers from different faiths have referred to it. Jewish students, for example, have emphasized it for years, pointing out that Jews who marry non-Jews often withdraw from their group, and that the children born to these mixed marriages are more prone to marry non-Jews. It is in this way that the Jews have been absorbed in large measure in China, Portugal, and Spain. Some Jewish writers insist that mixed marriages have robbed Jews of more adherents than have persecutions. Others stress the fact that often the most able and successful Jews are the ones that are most likely to make mixed marriages, and that their loss therefore is particularly serious. One Jewish writer, Maurice Fishberg, goes so far as to say that, of the great and talented Jews of the

past century, hardly any have left descendants within the fold of Judaism, and that the children born to Jews married to Christians are nearly all raised as Christians. Even the few that are raised as Jews are more apt to marry out of the faith than those born to Jews.

Catholic students have furnished rather definite evidence on the extent of leakage in their church resulting from mixed marriages. A factual study made for the Bishops' Committee on Mixed Marriages reported more than a decade ago that about 30 per cent of Catholic partners to such marriages were lost to the faith. Another study, reported by Father John L. Thomas, and published in 1956, based on large samples from various sections of the country, reports that, of the valid mixed marriages studied, about 25 per cent of the Catholic partners had lapsed in their practice of the faith, another 20 per cent attended church services only occasionally, and that but 55 per cent could be classified as fervent Catholics. Percentages of leakage vary from one parish to another, due to a variety of circumstances. One of these, particularly significant, shows that the relative leakage is lower when the wife is a Catholic than when she is a non-Catholic. Many reasons combine to explain this. Men often tend to defer to the wishes of their wives in such matters. The rearing of the children in the Catholic faith tends to be easier and more simple if the mother is a Catholic. When the mother is a non-Catholic, the difficulties in adhering to prenuptial agreements to rear the children as Catholics are greater, so that the temptation to withdraw from the Catholic church as a solution is much greater.

Several Protestant studies show similar degrees of leakage. Murray Leiffer, in a study of 743 mixed marriages, reports that, of a total of 444 men involved, 234, or 52 per cent, appear to have withdrawn from their churches, and of the

449 wives, 151, or approximately one-third, had done so. "Interfaith marriages," the author concludes, "accentuate what appears to be a dominant trend in urban life toward a disregard of things religious." Another study, by Judson Landis, a former president of the National Council on Family Relations, found that in 192 (55 per cent) of these cases, each spouse maintained his or her religion after marriage; and in 113 cases (33 per cent) either the Catholic or the Protestant changed to the faith of the other. In the remaining 41 marriages (12 per cent) Catholics had married a person of no religious faith. This study, it should be added, was made of the marital background of young people in college classes in a middle western university.

Further information on leakage due to mixed marriage is contained in the study made for the United Lutheran Church in America, to which reference has been made. According to data supplied by Lutheran pastors concerning the religious adjustment of Lutherans in 9,170 mixed marriages, it was found that in about 35 per cent of the cases each party retained its status in its respective church; in another 40 per cent of the cases the Lutheran member brought his or her mate into the Lutheran church; in about 10 per cent of the cases the Lutheran left his or her church to join the church of the non-Lutheran; and in the remaining 15 per cent of the cases both mates dropped out of the church or their religious adjustment was not known.

This study would indicate a relatively high degree of persistence of the Lutheran faith in the case of mixed marriages, a fact that is borne out in the data gathered by sociologist Murray Leiffer. That study showed that Roman Catholics and Lutherans were less prone to leave their church than were other groups.

Moreover, the leakage which results from mixed marriages appears to be cumulative. Mixed marriages breed leakage, and in two ways. First, many of the children born to mixed marriages are sure to be lost to the church of one of the parents, and frequently are lost to the churches of both, either because they join a neutral church or affiliate with none. Secondly, the children resulting from mixed marriages tend to make mixed marriages in turn. More adequate discussion of these points is reserved for a later chapter.

2. A second reason for church objection to mixed marriages is their interference with religious observances. All religious groups, as has been pointed out, have ritualistic requirements which reach into the daily lives of their members. Many of these center in, or involve, family living. The older, stronger, and more firmly organized religions particularly emphasize such rituals, knowing full well that people can best be held together by doing things together. Mixed marriages interfere with their observances, and thus weaken the religious life of their members. A Roman Catholic or a Methodist, for example, who marries outside of his church, tends to find it more difficult, because of such a marriage, to become or remain a good Catholic or Methodist. Even where there may be no cessation of, or interference with, such observances, the situation may result in an intangible diminution of interest or fervor.

The possible importance of these rituals in this connection may be illustrated in a reference to them by Maurice Fishberg, a Jewish writer to whom we have previously referred. "Certain rituals, especially the dietary laws," he writes, "have made marriage outside the pale of Judaism almost impossible. When men and women cannot partake a meal at one table, they cannot become intimately acquainted; and as long as there is no intimate social contact, there can be no marriage. The student of social science who carefully examines the facts will inevitably arrive at the conclusion that as long as the Jews adhere to their religious practices, and rigidly observe the dietary laws, no marriages between them and those of other faiths can take place."

3. Most religions, perhaps all of them, look upon marriage and the family as a special province of their interest and control. Historically this has been the case, and logically there is every reason to justify it. Religious worship and the living of a good life as prescribed by the church can best develop and flourish in terms of family units and unity. The family as a unit, both in this world and in the life to come, is the ideal of all the religions represented in this country. If only a fraction of what every expert in the field of family life says about the role of the family in determining the thought and behavior of its members is true, then obviously no individual member's religious life can be divorced from the life and thought of its other members. Moreover, the rearing of children, which is a prime function of the family, is the basis of church maintenance and growth, and the direction and emphases of that rearing are related in many ways to the values stressed by religious teaching.

4. Finally, every churchman, in the course of his pastoral work, comes to learn of the lives of his people and what factors influence their development. Any kind of work with people is a school in human behavior, building up a reservoir of experience which gives insight and determines judgment. This slow accumulation of experience may be just as scientific in its method, and in some ways more sound in its conclusions, as the latest techniques of the ivory-towered experts. From the conclusions of its individual workers,

every religion builds up a vast store of collective experience which comes to express itself in general policies, administrative emphases, and canonical requirements.

It is in this way, over long periods of time, that all of our religions have come to see the frequent dangers to family unity and stability resulting from interfaith marriages. Alongside of their conclusions in this respect are the findings which are presented in the next several chapters.

LAY REACTIONS TO CHURCH OPPOSITION

Thus far we have tried to present the church view toward mixed marriages, and the reasons for these views. It seems proper to add the reactions of selected types of laymen to these views. Four such lines of argument will be presented.

First, the answer of some lay critics to the churches' opposition is that they are largely or wholly selfish and self-centered, that they are thinking only of their membership strength and their financial sinews, and the effects that mixed marriages will have upon them. At first glance, certain of the facts support these charges. Churchmen do see the problem of leakage from theirs to other churches, but they also see additions in return from the same source. And churchmen's interest in their growth is not entirely a numerical and/or financial one. Most clergymen, we think, may be trusted to have wider interests than their immediate self-interests. Perhaps the charge leveled against the clergy here is the same that one hears about any professional group, and the answer in each case is the same.

Next, the charge is made at times that the church creates the problems of mixed marriages by its very opposition to them. "The reason a mixed marriage breaks up," storms a contemporary gladiator, "is because of the strain put upon it by the church leaders and the religious groups involved. If it weren't for the stigma that they attach to such a marriage, it would present no problems at all. Divorce doesn't result when a New York boy marries a Philadelphia girl, because no one is reminding them all the time in one way or another of the terrible thing they have done."

By way of reply, it may be said that here again there is a glimmer of truth, in that the opposition of one's church to a mixed marriage cannot be said as a rule to be helpful. The charge as a whole, however, misses the point of the nature of interfaith marriages as set forth in Chapter 2, and our repeated emphases that a mixed marriage that is significant as such is one where the differences are cultural rather than superficially ceremonial. Church opposition may accentuate, but it does not create, the fundamental differences.

A third reaction, sometimes expressed and more often implied, is that religion and the church are no longer important —at least, not important enough to be considered in so personal and serious a matter as choice of a lifelong mate. This is a secular age, an age of change, dominated by science, we are told. It is science that is the architect of our civilization. Its achievements dominate modern culture, and its spirit shapes the character of our intellectual as well as our spiritual life. To many contemporary persons, all other expressions of human intelligence are somewhat futile. The final appeal in all problems and points of disputation is to the scientist, and his judgments are thought to be true and righteous altogether. In this brave new world, say the bright young minds, religion is passé. Science, as a recent writer reminded us, is a sacred cow.

Accepting this point of view for the moment, although there are many persons who do not, the question then comes to be: What does science say about mixed marriages? The next several chapters will attempt to give the answer which social scientists are beginning to make. Suffice it to say that the scientists may oppose mixed marriages as much, or even more, than do the churchmen.

Finally, in contrast to the foregoing somewhat critical reactions, is a more friendly one which accepts, even if grudgingly at times, the rightness and necessity of the church's position. Church policy, it is conceded, rests on a knowledge of many cases. It is a collective judgment, based on centuries of human experience, and, as Will Durant once put it, only modern youth knows better than the verdict of twenty centuries.

Certain thoughtful persons go farther than this. They see the necessity for the religious control of human conduct in an area larger than that of family life. They point out that historically man has always subjected his actions to the will of the gods, as interpreted for him, and that these controls have succeeded when and where others have failed. And not only has the religious sanction or rejection of forms of conduct been an effective one historically, but the need for it is greater today than at many other times in the past, for today, especially in our urban centers of population, some of the oldest and most powerful controls of conduct have weakened or have largely disappeared.

The case of the changing role of the neighborhood is an illustration in point. The old-fashioned neighborhood, where everybody knew everybody and knew most things about all its people, served a very important role in regard to behavior. It not only defined what was acceptable behavior and what was not, but it brought tremendous pressure upon its members to conform. Originally, the neighborhood was the whole world of its members, and who could withstand its pressures? Moreover, these pressures covered the widest range—talk, shouts, mimicry, gossip, epithets, ridicule, avoidance, fear, shame, and praise. "What will the neighbors say?"

Today, in our cities, with their polyglot of peoples, moving in and out, this kind of neighborhood seldom exists. The city is a place of anonymity: one may not know his neighbors, not even by name, after years of close residence. Certainly, the neighborhood and its pressures are largely passé, and its passing leaves a large void in the controls of conduct. Does not this passing of the external controls of conduct throw increased responsibilities upon those within the individual, and does not this imply a greater role and a stronger need for religion than ever before? Certainly the advocates of this point of view have much on their side.

To summarize this part of our discussion, we have tried to show that all religious bodies, like all closely knit and integrated groups, are concerned with the behavior of their members, especially in matters that affect their relations to their groups. Naturally, then, they are opposed to the marriage of their members with persons of another religious faith. Chief among the reasons for this are the threat of such marriages to church membership, their interference with religious observances, and their disorganizing effect upon family life and child rearing. Lay reactions to this church interest vary from strong opposition to deep-seated respect and appreciation.

CHAPTER SIX

Husband and Wife

The foregoing chapters have dealt with a number of subjects which concern people contemplating a mixed religious marriage. Ultimately, though, such people want to know: "What will a marriage like this mean to *ME*, and to my husband or wife?" To that question this chapter is devoted. It does not offer categorical answers. It cannot give three easy steps to success in such a marriage. It will not predict inevitable failure. Its aim is to present the facts of what has happened to some people who have made interfaith marriages and who have seen fit to communicate the results, and to add the sociological interpretation of why those results occur in our own society at this particular time. The emphasis in this chapter is on problems. This does not mean that interfaith marriage cannot possibly be happy. It means that chances of individual happiness are greater if the problems are faced squarely, even though that should sometimes result in a decision not to marry. The last chapter in the book will deal with the already-married and the adjustment techniques that have been described by people who have contracted interfaith marriages.

MATE SELECTION AND INTERFAITH MARRIAGE

Most marriages in the United States come about in the same way. Two young people fall in love with each other, feel that they were made for each other, and that they cannot live without each other. This is so normal with us that it seems unnecessary to make such a statement. It is not the norm, however, throughout the history of mankind. It is much more usual that brides and grooms have been selected for each other by parents, kinsfolk, or marriage-makers. To Americans, this seems like the worst possible kind of infringement on individual rights. Nevertheless, a brief consideration of the two systems of mate selection may serve to bring into focus some of the problems inherent in our own.

Mixed religious marriages occur most often within our system, and seldom in the more traditional one. When older people do the selecting of marital partners they stress cultural similarity between the two. In part, this is so because, out of long experience, adults have come to see that marriage is not an island on which a bride and groom isolate themselves. Marriage is just a small segment of family, kinsfolk, neighbors, friends, community, nation, and society as a whole. The individual couple is a part of all these, whether or not it wishes to be. It and they impinge upon each other inevitably. Thus, when the elders make the marriage, they consider the importance of the couple's being able to share all of these things with common points of view and common ways of behaving. This is the type of marriage which took place in the traditional Chinese family—a stable institution for thousands of years, until recently influenced to some extent by Western civilization.

With us, though, both the privilege and the responsibility of marital selection are put into the hands of the individuals concerned. For the most part, they are young and not very experienced, though they often feel more sure of themselves than they ever have in their lives. Also, they are almost always deeply in love, an emotion which is certainly essential to the finest type of marriage as Americans conceive of it. The combination, though, of romantic love and inexperience can be very blinding for a time, the time during which young people are making one of the most important decisions of their whole lives. In our individualistic way, we have devised very few means of helping people to think clearly and to see objectively during this crucial period. "Interference" from family and friends in the choice of a mate is so intolerable that it as frequently produces stubbornness as thoughtfulness. No. The couple must somehow accomplish this important thing by itself.

How Well Do We Know Ourselves and Others?

Current books advising those about to be married almost uniformly insist that the couple should face its differences with "reason." This means talking out with each other their feelings about many things. For our purpose, it means their feelings about both of their religions and how they are going to adjust. How much does religion mean to each one? What will they do about the observance of Holy Days, about dietary habits? How do they feel about children, limitation of family size, the education and religious training of children? Though the books give wise counsel, these "reasoned conferences" are not always successful. The emotion of love is riding high; everything else is secondary to it. Religion, observances, and the long-distant education of children have, perhaps, never seemed so dull and unimportant. "And anyway, we can take care of those things as we go along."

Once the desired goal of marriage has been achieved, however, other aspects of life begin to reassume their former importance in the whole value scheme of life. What has happened, then, is that the individuals who have reasoned, have not reasoned at all. They have submerged certain emotional values beneath the value of their love for each other. Instead of accomplishing understanding, they have fooled and deprived themselves.

Then, too, the fact must be faced that there are people who will reason in any direction to achieve success. The man who asked his fiancée how many children she wanted was acting "according to the book." He showed no resistance when she answered, "Six." He, however, wanted none, and felt perfectly sure that once married he could change his fiancée's mind. This is a rather drastic example. Yet many people who get married have a few things in mind that they are waiting to "correct" in their mates, once they are married. This is a dangerous philosophy. People are hard to change. Usually they do not want to, and are quite stubborn about suggestions to that effect. In such cases the conference has resulted not only in the individual's fooling himself, but in deceiving his partner as well.

An excellent illustration of these two possibilities of misunderstanding is found in a marriage counseling case concerning the engagement of a Jewish girl to an Irish Catholic boy.[1] The two had decided that neither one was strong in religious faith and that each one respected the faith of the other. They were, they said to each other, liberal-minded adults who could permit each other this difference. Because the girl's father heatedly opposed the intended marriage, she consented to see a counselor. The counselor recalled

[1] Maurice J. Karpf, "Marriage Counseling and Psychotherapy," *Marriage and Family Living*, XIII, 4 (1951), 169-74.

that this girl had formerly been quite upset because her younger brother had not taken the cause of Judaism seriously, and she had tried to make him see his responsibility toward his own people. Now, she herself was denying them by saying that her religion was not very important. What, the counselor asked, was her true attitude? Had she really changed her mind, or was this opportunism? Did she know that she would have to rear her children in a faith that she was unwilling to take as her own? This seemed to shock the girl. Her shock revealed to her counselor both that her religious feelings went deeper than she had admitted to herself and that her fiancé had not told her of the requirements of his church. Subsequent talks between the engaged couple showed clearly that the young man's religious feeling, too, was not quite as he had pictured it. He expected to marry within the dictates of his church, and had felt all along that when his fiancée took the instructions she would see the value of the Catholic religion, turn to it, and solve their one problem. When, in anger, she assured him that she would never become a Catholic, he accused her of having misrepresented the strength of her own religious feelings. Her love turned to extreme bitterness and a sense of injustice done her until she was led to take an honest look at her own role in this maze of misrepresentations.

The behavior of these two young people who were in love was not particularly unique. They were merely acting like two average human beings caught in the web of mixed emotions. Had they married, what might their life have been like? A British psychiatrist, Dr. Eliot Slater, and a psychiatric social worker, Moya Woodside, studied the marital relations of two hundred urban working-class families in London. They point out that numerous hostilities affect human societies and that they are focused on differences between conflicting groups. Each group considers its way superior. Real value does not enter the picture. Reason is "swamped" by emotion of a primitive level—hostility. We add that love, also, is an emotion which is primitive in its basic nature. Such primitive emotions are fierce and difficult to control by reason. In an interfaith marriage, where the cultures are quite different, these two emotions are at war with each other. The question is, which is the stronger in any individual marriage? If the analogy to war is justified, it might be pointed out that at present, in war, there is no real victory and no real defeat—just periods of cessation from open warfare. So, in such a marriage, the individual's own inner feelings of love and hostility may be in a continuous process of armistice and battle.

This is one of the costs that ought to be given consideration before an interfaith marriage is contracted. The individual alone has to decide whether this particular marriage is so important as to be worth that price—but it may be difficult for him to know the proper answer until it is too late.

THE PERSONALITIES OF THOSE WHO MAKE OUT-MARRIAGES

It may be of interest to know something about the people who marry outside their religious faith. What are they like? Are they special kinds of people? The studies which have attempted to discover this concern only Jewish-Gentile marriage. The finding of Drs. Slotkin and Resnik are summarized here. They are:

1. The unorganized or demoralized person, a product of the deteriorated areas of cities where people do not conform to the cultural standards of the larger society.
2. The promiscuous person, who looks outside his own group for casual contacts that sometimes lead to marriage.

3. The adventurous person, who is stimulated by the new and different.
4. The detached person, cut off from his own group and with little opportunity to marry within it.
5. The rebellious person, who turns against his own culture and defiantly adopts another.
6. The marginal person, who marries for superior status for himself or children and who remains marginal to both his own and the new group.
7. The acculturated person, who has come to value the characteristics of the dominant group as superior.
8. The emancipated person, who has lost those traits of his own group that are an obstacle to intermarriage.

One gets the picture of a kind of person who is not deeply rooted in his own cultural setting. He has been torn up, or has torn himself up, from it for a variety of reasons. A study of American-Japanese marriages shows much the same thing. At the University of Chicago, under the sponsorship of the Family Study Center and the Race Relations Center, Dr. Anselm Strauss has examined the data on such marriages. He reports that the young people involved were of marriageable age, yet with no romantic ties to anyone of their own race. They were relatively independent of family, neither supporting nor being supported by them. They were earning their own living at a "job," but they were not long-run, career-minded people. They were not "joiners" of social, recreational, or religious organizations. Again, one sees the absence of roots among their own kind. The identification of such types in other forms of out-marriage would be interesting, but such studies are not available.

Just from the most casual observations of young people who are making mixed religious marriages, however, it seems obvious that they do not all really fit into the pattern of rootlessness. Still another fact about our contemporary society may account for their turning to a member of an outgroup. In America, adolescence tends to become a period of rebellion against established authority. We keep young people caged by family and other institutions, long after they are physically ready to fly. Tensions are apt to spring up between the youth and his "keeper." Not all adolescents feel this way; but if ever a person is to develop a rebellion against his family and all it stands for, it is apt to be during the teens and the early twenties, and to be stronger at that time than ever again. Actually, the usual experience is that it wears itself out rather promptly, once freedom is attained, and the opposite tendency starts—the slow but sure growing appreciation of one's family as one gets older and becomes family-minded one's self.

Many a marital tragedy can be accounted for in this way. The greatest antagonism toward authority and family happens, in America, to come simultaneously with mate selection. In fact, albeit unwittingly, a boy or girl in rebellion may select a mate more in a spirit of defiance against the family than of real love for the person selected. If the person is quite unlike the family, then one can tear off those binding roots. The roots are strong, though, and they start growing again.

THE DECISION IS MADE

After careful consideration, a couple decides to enter into an interfaith marriage. Immediately there are matters of a practical nature that must be attended to.

The families have to be informed. Will they mind? If they do, what will it mean to the couple? Here are some of the answers as they have been told to us. "There was a question raised in this couple's premarital discussions. How would his family react toward marriage with a Gentile? The wife-to-be knew that many Jews, especially those of the Orthodox and Conservative churches, consider such a marriage a disgrace. The answer was that . . . it would not affect him. However, on two occasions after plans to introduce his fiancée to some members of his family, they were canceled because he didn't know how they would treat her and he didn't want her hurt." Thus, introductions were postponed until after marriage. The problem was shelved, but it grew in proportion before it again saw the light of day. In another case, the Baptist and Quaker parents of the couple both tried so hard to proselytize the member of the opposite faith that the young couple ran away and were married in a civil ceremony. Again, a Protestant boy found his family so unalterably opposed to his union with a Catholic girl, and her family so receptive of him, that he postponed his marriage until he could join the Catholic church and be married within it. Already, forces outside themselves were necessitating decisions they had not foreseen and had not intended to make.

Then, whether or not families take the proposed marriage in stride, the marriage itself must be arranged. Where shall it take place? If the marriage is between an Orthodox Jew and a Gentile, or between a Catholic and a Protestant, the couple cannot be married by the usual synagogue or church ceremony. If, however, the Orthodox Jew or the Catholic marries in some other ceremony, he is not considered by his church to be married, nor are his children considered legitimate. Should the Protestant, then, change to the religion of his mate to solve this problem? A young Jewish girl did this in order to marry the man she loved. Years later, he said to her with bitterness: "You'll never change a Jew into a Catholic or a Catholic into a Jew. It is like dipping a chicken into water and pulling him out. He still remains a chicken."

Once the marriage is arranged, who is to be invited to the wedding? Can the families and friends from both sides be depended upon to help make this a happy occasion, or must the guests be carefully selected? Who can be chosen as attendants? A girl writes: "I shall never forget being excluded from my cousin's wedding because I, a non-Catholic, could not participate in the wedding. The parish priest was a strict one, and insisted on the entire wedding party being Roman Catholic. I was young enough to want to be a member of the wedding, yet not quite old enough to understand why, as a non-Catholic, I could not be a junior bridesmaid. Second cousins, who were Catholics, were in the wedding group but none was so close to my cousin as I was. My cousin seemed quite upset by the entire thing, but it was law she must be married in her own parish. It fairly broke my heart."

The joining of two families in matrimony frequently presents difficulties like those mentioned above. When there is a religious barrier between the two, a new dimension is added. Families tend to regard the marriage of their members as religious sacraments, and want their own kind. Planning for an interfaith marriage can, then, be attended by a great deal of tension, and may require very careful calculation in order to prevent permanently injured family relationships.

NOW THEY ARE MAN AND WIFE

The wedding is past, and the couple leave for the honeymoon. Now they have escaped from any of the pressures that may have been visited upon them before. That is over and done with, and they can really begin their life together peacefully in the manner they had formerly discussed with each other. This is the beginning of the reality-testing of their plans.

Because of the nature of courtship and mate selection in our society, almost all brides and grooms learn things about their mates that they had never even thought about before. Dating and courting situations are rather artificial. They involve parties and dancing, socializing with friends, with some time saved for each other for love-making and "getting to know each other better," at which times each one is putting his very best foot forward lest the engagement be endangered. Now, overnight, the two are enclosed in a total life situation with each other alone. It suddenly becomes very intimate and all-inclusive. Every person who has ever married has discovered in his mate some little domestic habits that were surprising because they were so different from his own—obviously, because they have been reared differently and have had different life experiences. No two people are just alike. It matters a great deal, though, whether these surprises are endearing, neutral, or repulsive. The following examples from our case records are selected to illustrate difficulties that arose, not because of general personality differences, but because of religious-cultural ones.

The role of religion in sexual behavior has been discussed in Chapter 2. Kinsey's findings were substantiated in our records. Attitudes toward the sex act and techniques used were frequently at variance. In one case, the problem was more concrete. For reasons which they both considered wise, a Catholic girl and her Protestant groom had decided to use contraceptives for a period of two years. Faced with the reality of it, all the strength of her religious training came to the fore. She could not commit this sin. There developed between them a sort of compromise in which sometimes he insisted upon contraceptives and at other times she would rebel against them. The result was that, when she had her way, he was worried; when he had his, she was overcome with guilt. It was wholly unsatisfactory for both.

A young woman who had been brought up in a high church tradition of stern, individual responsibility toward one's family was appalled when she discovered that her husband's total, and small savings were being used up on the honeymoon. Upon discussing with him the new responsibilities for themselves and their future children, she reported, he declaimed against her materialistic attitude, and said, "As the Lord provides, so we shall live."

Finally, the following complaints came from a Jewish groom and a Gentile bride, quite independently of each other. He thought it revolting and quite inconsiderate that, after two days of honeymooning at a hotel, his wife ordered ham for dinner. He half-suspected that she had done it deliberately. She confessed that she had never noticed how he talked before they were married, but then she became uncomfortably aware of the clipping of "g's" and "t's" and the "Molly Goldberg inflection."

In many cases, of course, the honeymoon is a delightful and happy time. It is that little island to themselves that they had been longing for. When it is over, they are eager to go home and settle down. Then, they discover that they will never again be so alone together. All sorts of people and things begin entering that tight little partnership. The rest of this chapter concerns itself with selected aspects of life as they affect the continuing interfaith marriage.

FRIENDSHIPS

The average healthy person does not like to make a hermitage out of his own home. People like to have friends, just for companionship's sake. Also, if they are happy and proud of their mates and homes, they like to share them and show them. Ordinarily, this is one of the exciting parts of getting married—having your own place, being unrestricted as to frequency and timing and type of entertaining, and having whom you please without parental regulation or censure. To be able to share friends in recreation, to have them to depend upon in trouble, even to be able to talk about them after they have gone home, are things that enrich married life and give a couple just one more satisfaction in common. They also prevent them from becoming ingrown and self-centered.

People contemplating marriage may overlook this part of their future lives together because, above all else, they want to be alone. What difference does it make if he doesn't get along with her friends; nor she, with his; nor their friends, with each other? They are marrying each other, not their friends.

A sociologist, Dr. Judson Landis, who has made many studies of marital relationships, has said that there are certain areas of living that create particular difficulties in marital adjustment. One of these concerns relationships with mutual friends. He finds that, among couples who have been married an average of twenty years and who have never been separated nor divorced, 76.4 per cent found satisfaction in this area from the beginning of married life, and 7.9 per cent never did. On the average, if such satisfaction were not found from the start, it took six years of "trying" until adjustment was made. During this time, then, these couples were missing the very constructive pleasure of sharing mutual friends, and at a time, in the beginning of married life, when the responsibilities of home-making are light, and when, after children come along, the wife is rather tied down and needs refreshing, relaxing association with other people of her own age.

In an interfaith marriage, there are unique and special factors that may cause less satisfaction and greater conflict as far as friends are concerned. Perhaps the couple has married thinking that religion is not too important because both are "tolerant" individuals. Do their friends feel the same way? Not everyone has the same attitude toward freedom in social relationships. Some people socialize readily across all kinds of cultural lines. Others do not. If a selective process among one's own friends begins to appear, how is it rationalized? Some of them may have to be counted off, with a few pangs, as not being true friends, as being bigoted. If the loss is great, however, it takes a strong person to withstand the gradual feeling that this has happened because of what my husband or my wife is.

What sorts of friends do married people usually choose? Dr. Carle Zimmerman of Harvard University and his associate, Dr. Broderick, say that people choose friends very much like themselves. In their study of a city where most of the inhabitants were new, and thus had to seek out new friends, it was found that a very high proportion of them made their closest friendships with people who were similar in regional origin, income group, and religion. Furthermore, there was a relationship between similarity of friends and both divorce and delinquency. There were fewer cases of these in families whose friends resembled them. The authors interpreted this as a result of the strength of common values in a "compromise world," starting in the family with marriage and extending outward in social space. If this is true, the interfaith marriage is handicapped. The partners' life values are different. Each has his own friends, and his values are different. If the couple has children, what values do they take? This, however, is part of the story of the next chapter.

The people who have made this book possible by contributing their stories speak very emphatically about the matter of mutual friends. When the cultural gap is wide, there is always some "adjusting" necessary. It takes three forms. One is to alternate in friendships and never to mix the groups. Another is to cut off the friends of one of the spouses and hold to the other's. The third is to leave old friends behind and make new ones. Over and over again, when this is done, the comment is: "We have made our friendships with people like ourselves who have also made mixed marriages." An exceedingly defensive woman, during an interview, said: "I can't see why all this fuss about interfaith marriage. *All* my friends have made them and we all get along fine." When asked if it weren't a little strange that all her friends happened to have made these marriages, the defenses gave way completely. She smiled, rather bitterly, and said: "Of course. The fact is that you cannot even speak the same language unless you are a member of 'the club'."

"Private Life"

A problem that has appeared to become troublesome in the daily life routine of certain married couples is a result of their having different ideas about the extent to which the church has authority over the individual's so-called private life and differences in observances involved. This is a matter quite apart from the depth of one's devotion to God.

Churches vary widely in respect to authority over their members—and in which areas of their lives. The Roman Catholic church is often accused of being *the* authoritarian religion, but this is not wholly true.[2] There is a vast difference, for example, between the Orthodox and the Reformed Jewish religion in this respect. Within the general category of Orthodox, there are many sects, some of which are so strict that man and wife may not sleep together in a double bed, and the wife may not leave her home without first covering her head with a wig. Even the protesting Protestants have sects of varying degrees of protestation. As was suggested in Chapter 2, some forbid smoking, card playing, and drinking; others prescribe certain ways of dressing; still others seem to have the attitude that, if they can catch you for the Sunday service long enough to remind you of your religious responsibility, then they had better interfere no further.

It is quite true that the differences between the most protesting Protestant and a Jewish sect similar to the one just described are so great as almost to preclude intermarriage, but the case of Roger and Myra (in Chapter 2) serves to illustrate that, where the differences are less obvious and spectacular, marriages do occur. When they do, the marital partners have their own attitudes, in which they have been indoctrinated by family and church and by which they have been living from their earliest years. It is relatively easy to be "tolerant" about an opposing attitude until it interferes

----

[2] A very devout young Catholic woman described to us the changes in attitudes toward authority as she and her family moved from parish to parish. In the urban, upper-class parishes, the priests attended to their church duties, made calls, but demanded little from the parishioners. In rural, lower- and middle-class parishes, the priests were a regular part of family life. She reported that many details of their most intimate routines changed as they moved from one parish to another.

with one's convictions about how to live one's own life. Then it becomes a different matter. As a novelist has put it: "When you eat breakfast with a woman, what she believes colors her conversation with you and affects your day, and you and your beliefs affect her."[3]

The following are some examples of contrasting attitudes, based on the extent of the church's authority over family life:

Three small children, a Catholic, an Anglican, and a Methodist, got to wrangling, as children will, about whose things were "best." When they came to religion, the Catholic and the Anglican had the little Methodist cornered. They explained that their churches were the best because they had early morning masses. Mommy and Daddy could go to them, be back before breakfast, and have the rest of the day for themselves. The little Methodist repaired to his mother, nearly in tears. His mother assured him that all of Sunday was God's special day and that to crowd Him into the most convenient time in order to get it over with was definitely wicked.

Or, one can point to the Protestant bride whose Catholic groom arose on the first Sunday of their honeymoon to go to early mass. She would not have been more hurt had he slapped her in the face, and she could never understand what seemed to her a lack of sensitivity and gallantry.

Again, in a Jewish-Methodist intermarriage between two busy professional people, the husband and wife both kept stolidly to their own religions. They discovered that the one time they could have shared activities together—weekends—was made difficult for them. The day that she considered the time for recreation and leisure was his Sabbath.

[3] Robert Raynolds, *The Sinner of Saint Ambrose* (New York: Bobbs-Merrill Co., 1952), p. 195.

The same was true for him. They had only a brief period on Saturday evenings for companionable socializing with each other and with their friends. They both felt deprived when they saw how much more time together other couples had. That was the way it had to be, though, and it has continued.

A young groom with a healthy male appetite, who was used to a late, leisurely, and large Sunday breakfast before church, found that his bride fasted until she returned home from her services. He did not like to make it more difficult for her by asking her to prepare a meal for him. He did not like to eat it alone, anyway. So he "grabbed a bite" after she had left and before he went to church. He said he had never realized what his family meal and trip to church together had meant to him, nor how much he had unconsciously been projecting them into his images of married life. Sunday, formerly a special day, now seemed all wrong.

More obvious are the family problems that grow out of differing religious holidays. One woman writes: "Christmases are celebrated as they were in the wife's household and her family helps to celebrate them. Easters are a combination. The father observes the dietary laws of the Passover. Mother and child do not."

Several other thought-provoking problems came to light in our case records. A young man whose business was books, who was an avid reader and who enjoyed discussing the contents, was infuriated when he discovered that his wife would not open a book he brought home until she knew whether or not her church approved it. She tried to explain why this was so, but he could never see any other point of view than that this was the worst kind of meddling in a purely private affair. The epithets he heaped upon her church were colorful, and they did not pale as time went on and the subject came up again and again.

Finally, attitudes toward how much of a couple's income is due the church vary from one sect to another. Some churches politely "suggest," but with no real pressure; others have "drives" periodically, to whip up the emotions to give; still others teach the practice of tithing as a definite religious responsibility. In our cases, this caused annoyance, especially when the bread-winning husband refused to go along with the wife's tithing habits. She felt the responsibility; he earned the money and dispensed it; and there was little she could do about it.

Perhaps these illustrations seem picayune—just little things that mature people can work out and take in stride. It is just as well to remember, though, that marriage is not merely a matter of handling great big crises. It is made up, for the most part, of the little things concerned in everyday living, which repeat themselves endlessly day after day and year after year. The wheels of matrimony turn round and round over much the same course, and the less grit they acquire on the way the smoother is the journey.

A Child Is Born

Perhaps all the problems discussed so far have been minimal for the married couple. They have been able to adjust to such difficulties and have been very happy together. Now, husband and wife become father and mother.

It is not easy to understand what a child means until a living baby is born. Then, suddenly, you see a part of your own flesh and blood. It belongs to you as nothing else ever has. It is a greater responsibility, too, because it is so completely helpless and dependent upon its parents. It is not only physically helpless; it depends upon them to answer the questions of what is the proper way to live in order to

achieve happiness in this world and immortality thereafter.
If mother and father agree on these subjects, the child has
no questions and feels secure. Mother and father have no
questions, either. If their religious philosophies are in opposition, however, how will they feel?

She is a Catholic. She fell in love with a Protestant and
married him. He agreed to comply with the dictates of her
faith because he wanted so much to marry her. Now there
is a baby. The baby is as much his son as hers. Must he keep
his hands off the religious, educational, and cultural training
of his own son, and, if so, at what price to the family relationship?

He is a Baptist who fell in love with a Jewish girl. The
love was so strong that it was easy to iron out all possible
problems by intellectualizing. Now there is a baby. About
him, the father feels emotional, not intellectual. Does he
really feel happy about having him reared in the Jewish
faith? Would his mother feel happy about having him reared
in the Baptist faith?

If the records that provide the material for this book are
of any value, they indicate that parental feelings supersede
romantic love and individualism. People may marry without
too much thought about family, but when a family arrives
they feel both protective and possessive about it.

THE TIME PERSPECTIVE

A great many books about marriage give the impression
that it is something that happens to young people, that early
adjustment may be difficult but is important, and that is the
end of the story. It is far from the end, however. The fact
is that marriages age, and people and conditions change.

This is an unpopular subject with young people, and

understandably so. When one is fourteen, the graduating senior seems like a man-or-woman-of-the-world. To the Freshman in college, the forty-year-old "alum" seems practically defunct. Youth is the time! The feelings of such old folks cannot be imagined by the young, nor do they really think they themselves will reach that stage. Or, if they think about it at all, it is to be pretty sure that by that time nothing will matter too much, because the best of life will be over anyway and they will be resigned to the rest. How can they be expected to think otherwise, with our society's emphasis on youth?

Nevertheless, in the modern world, with its wonderful advances in medicine and hygiene, people are living longer, keeping younger, and feeling healthier. The average person of fifty today is a very different physical specimen from the one in 1800. He is a different mental specimen, too. Being physically able in a society that stresses the individual pursuit of happiness, he is quite unwilling to adhere to the philosophy that the best of life is over. He is as eager and able to enjoy it now as he ever has been.

This puts an extra burden on youth in mate selection, and a heavy burden. To make a marriage that will endure forever and be happy, one has to choose a partner who will "wear well" for generations and who will do so despite changes of all kinds. Any factor in a marriage which indicates that with time and crises the partners might change in different directions and not together, is one that should be considered seriously. A difference in faith can be one such factor.

For example, here is the story of a non-Catholic girl who marries a Catholic boy. He has explained his church's stand in regard to the sex relationship. She loves children, wants a large family, and is quite ready to accept the philosophy of her husband. Their sex adjustment is entirely satisfactory, and she proves to be very fertile. Six "little steps" are born to them. From the third one on, the births grow increasingly more difficult. For the birth of the sixth child, she insists upon going to a non-Catholic hospital because she has heard from her friends that she will be permitted more relief from the pains of delivery. At this point, her husband looks at her as though she had a new face. His mother bore ten children without complaint. Something must suddenly have gone wrong with his wife's attitude toward child bearing and with her faith. She is adamant, however, and he is embarrassed for her. He hates to tell his friends, and particularly his family, because this seems to indicate a weakness in his formerly perfect wife—a weakness he is all too loath to report, since they had warned him against marrying a non-Catholic.

After the delivery in a nonsectarian hospital, her obstetrical surgeon advises her not to have any more children. Her older sister, the mother of two youngsters, comes to visit her, looking chic and svelte in a new fur coat, exclaims over the baby, and says: "Now, look, Beth. It is just about time you stopped or you'll be physically depleted and financially on the rocks." Beth's husband's family is concerned over her condition, too, and they are very kind and helpful; but they make no suggestions about limiting her family. Confused, she gets a feeling that they don't really care about her very much, and are not interested in her individual welfare. For six long days, while recovering, she thinks and broods. When she gets back home, she tells her husband that she cannot face pregnancy again. He is gentle and understanding and considerate, knowing that she has been through an ordeal. For five months there is no sex relationship at all. Then the subject can no longer be evaded.

He offers to send her to a good doctor to learn the principles of rhythmic control. From the doctor she discovers that the identification of her individual rhythm will take some time, perhaps a year or more. Only then can he assure reasonable effectiveness. This seems intolerable to Beth, and she pours out her troubles to her sister, who answers: "It won't work anyway. Go get yourself fitted with a diaphragm. No one will know the difference." That, she is unwilling to do. So she speaks to her husband about the possibility, knowing all the time what his position will be and that she will be sympathetic with his honest convictions. For two years he continues to be considerate and careful of her. She does not get pregnant, but they lose their relaxed and wholly intimate relationship that had formerly meant so much to their marriage. She feels only fear. Finally, she can no longer face this careful and calculated distance from her husband, and does just what her sister suggested. Now, she is still living in fear—the fear of discovery that could result in her losing more than she has gained—and added to her fear is guilt over what she has done without her husband's knowledge.

Quite different is the story of a young man of Protestant faith and a Jewish college classmate who were married only after the most careful consideration of their possible problems. They consulted a marriage counselor as well as their own families and friends. They came to the conclusion that, since they lived in a community that did not look askance at such unions, and since he already had a job secured in that community, they would marry, but with two conditions understood. First, though each was not very active in his religion, each had a sense of identification with it that he felt was important. They would, then, go their separate ways religiously, but with mutual respect. The other condi-

tion was that they would have no children. The desire for
parenthood was not so strong in either of them as their
desire to make a life together. Realizing the problems that
the first condition to the marriage might make for children,
the couple decided against them.

Time seemed to prove that they had acted both with
reason and love, for they were happy with each other, their
families, and their mutual friends. Happiness often makes
for attractiveness and efficiency. It did in the case of this
young husband, and he was selected time after time for pro-
motions in his company. It looked as though he had every
opportunity to reach a high executive position at a relatively
early age. His business was a service-type organization in
which it was necessary for even the junior executives to
enter actively into the philanthropic, recreational, and religious life of the community. This he could effect easily, and
the charming couple was eagerly welcomed socially. The
fact that the wife did not share her husband's religious activities was completely understood. When the husband was
forty-two, he was called in for an interview by a member of
the board of directors who had been especially interested in
his career and personality. Another promotion was pending,
but he had gone as far as he could in his own branch office.
He was advised that in the community where the other office
was situated there was considerable feeling about marriages
like his. If his wife would not mind concealing her identity
and would accompany him in religious activities, continuing
opportunity would be theirs. He was confronted with three
possibilities. One was to try to persuade his wife, which he
would not do, and to which he felt sure she would not consent anyway. Another was to give up his job entirely and
look for another. The difficulties of finding another one to his
liking, at his advanced position, in a place where he could be

sure of acceptance for both of them, made this seem unwise to him. The alternative was to remain where he was, in happy social relationships, without promotion. This was his decision. It has resulted in putting a wedge between the couple that did not exist before, of frustration on his part, and self-consciousness on hers. Dissatisfaction is admitted by both of them as they watch the slow but steady progress of most of their friends who, the wife feels, are much less able than her own husband.

Unpredictable changes and emergencies occur in the aging of all marriages. They cannot be foreseen, and can be handled only as they arise. People with the same philosophy of life tend to react to them in the same way. Crises, even, may draw them closer together because they think and work in the same direction. The more diverse their attitudes the less is closeness apt to result from crises.

How Many Interfaith Marriages Succeed?

Problems are interesting and challenging. Americans like to hear about them, but have the spirited optimism to believe, "I could have solved that one. That couldn't happen to me." The information that is really wanted is, "How great are the chances for *success?*"

That is the most difficult question of all to answer, for no one knows. Failures are more easily counted because some of them come to the divorce courts and are on record. Even divorce does not tell the whole story, since it is clear that many families, interfaith or of one religion, live in states of constant warfare, tension, and unhappiness, and yet never break up. These cannot be counted either. Desertions and separations can be tabulated from records in certain places, but not very accurately. Furthermore, it has been pointed

out that desertions and separations do not always mean ultimate failure. A family may be reunited, and succeed the
second time; or, it may not. Two sociologists, interested in
the subject of interfaith marriage and its relative success,
studied the desertion and nonsupport records of 1,029 Philadelphia native white primary-marriage families for the year
1950. Drs. Monahan and Kephart found that the highest
rates of desertion and nonsupport were in families where
the wife was Catholic and the husband Protestant. Slightly
lower were the rates for families in which the wife was
Protestant and the husband Catholic. Other types of mixed
religious marriages showed a much lower percentage of desertion and nonsupport. This looks very much as if these
rates vary with attitudes toward divorce and the ease or
difficulty of obtaining one—especially since the same study
shows the percentage for both partners Catholic in that same
year to be higher than all the others cited here. It is obvious,
then, that available information on desertion cannot help
much toward answering the question of success. The divorce
rate is the only evidence left. Here is the story that it tells.

In a study by Judson Landis of 4,108 marriages of parents of college students in Michigan, the divorce rates were
calculated by religion. It was found that when both partners
professed to having no religion, the rates were highest of all.
Next in order came the Catholic-Protestant marriages; then,
both Protestant; both Jewish; and both Catholic. A closer
look at the Catholic-Protestant divorce rate shows that if
the wife is the Protestant, divorce is apt to occur more than
twice as often than if the wife is Catholic.

To sum up this chapter briefly, mixed religious marriage
occurs most often where young people are permitted to
choose their own life partners when they are young and

romantically in love. Under such circumstances many young people who are not strongly rooted in their own family and religious groups, or are temporarily rebelling against them, choose a mate from outside their own group. The couple soon discovers that because of their two faiths there are decisions or compromises which must be made in respect to the wedding, sex behavior, finances, diet, friendships, the relation of church to home life, and religious holidays and observances. This deciding and compromising becomes more serious when a child is born, because a child cannot adopt two faiths and two ways of living. Sometimes, as marriages age, crises and changes occur to which the partners react differently because they have different philosophies of life. When this happens, crises may have the effect of making couples grow apart rather than together. Although present evidence is not altogether reliable, and usually tends to underestimate, it does indicate that failure in interfaith marriages is more frequent than in those of one faith.

CHAPTER SEVEN

When the Children Come

Marriage, it has been suggested, is considered by most young people to be strictly their own affair: a union between the two of them. About five out of every six marriages in the United States, however, produce children. Once married, people who make interfaith marriages seem to come to an understanding of what their marriage may mean for the children. Evidences of it appear in studies of childlessness and the birth rates of these families. A study made in Indianapolis, by Drs. Kiser and Whelpton, of couples who were almost past their childbearing years, showed that Protestant-Catholic couples had a higher rate of childlessness than either Protestant or Catholic couples. In the same city, the Protestant-Catholic birth rate was lower than the Catholic or the Protestant birth rate. There are a number of possible reasons for these low rates other than a conscious agreement between the couple on family limitation; but the rates do indicate some serious concern over the special problems of children, and because of children, that such marriages create. This chapter is concerned with some of those problems.

WHAT IS THE PURPOSE OF THE FAMILY?

Every human society has some kind of family system. Though the forms of these systems vary widely, they have universally two functions. They are the perpetuation of the group physically and culturally. In other words, every group desires to extend itself into the future by bearing children and caring for them so that they may live to grow up and produce other children. Just as important is the desire to rear those children in the ways of doing and thinking of the particular group. If this is not done, the society loses its identity. A people, for instance, who are proud to be Americans and who feel it is the best nation in the world, would not be satisfied just to bear children and then send them to Great Britain or Russia to be reared. They want their children to be Americans, to act and think like Americans, and not like Britishers nor Russians. Any group with pride in itself, that thinks its way of life is right, feels this way. It wants to pass its cultural heritage down to its children so that it will survive and so that the children will have the best possible heritage.

A religious group, as well as a nation, is a cultural group. A family in which parents are of different faiths cannot easily fulfil the function of cultural transmission. Which culture is to be handed down? Shall it be a mixture? Or both? Or neither? Presumably each parent has some feelings about his own heritage.

WHAT IS A FAMILY FROM THE CHILD'S POINT OF VIEW?

A child does not define his family in terms of its functions, but rather of his own feelings. It is, to him, a given number of people who do things to him and for him, and who tell him things. He is utterly dependent upon their acts for his survival and upon their love for his security and feeling of worth. As a matter of fact, some sociologists also define the family, not by its functions, but as a group of people who act with and upon each other. This sort of definition is, perhaps, more true to the child's eye than to society's. Recently, the family has been described as an "emotional organization," and the emotional atmosphere of one family was described thus: "My mother usually screams at us, the cat is always hungry, and the television gets turned off. We usually do something bad, and we are always spending money, and we don't get to see our father because we go to the Y so often and our Daddy isn't home. Only on Sunday is his day off."[1] This is how a child sees it, and within it he develops his own personality and behavior patterns.

Within this emotional organization of the family the child does not react emotionally the same way to all his family members—nor to outsiders, either. Some are warm, some pleasant, helpful, understanding, glamorous to him; others are the opposite of one or all of these things. Being relatively unaware of, and disinterested in, moral values, the small child tends to identify with the people to whom he is drawn because they are "nice" to him and he "likes" them, and to be repelled by those who are not and whom he does not like. He wants to be like the former (though from a moral point of view that person may be a jolly renegade) and avoids taking on the characteristics of the latter (who may be a veritable pillar of the community).

This is the case in all families. Where there is a cultural way, or a philosophy of life, that is common to all members of the family and kin groups, the differences that the child

[1] Gerald Handel and Robert D. Hess, "The Family as an Emotional Organization," *Marriage and Family Living*, XVIII, 2 (1956), 99.

sees among them will be mainly in terms of personality traits and gross behavior variances. He can adopt some and reject others in becoming himself, and yet stand as a person in unity with his whole family's cultural consensus. He is sure of the general route he must follow, and is only being selective of the particular roads he takes.

PERSONALITY IN A MIXED RELIGIOUS HOME

With the child of a mixed religious marriage, the case is different. His parents and their families represent two ways of life, often two opposing ways. He sees them being lived by people who are not equally attractive to him. Perhaps the following quotation will serve to illustrate how great a burden this can be to a child:

> My Jewish grandmother was the sweetest, most self-effacing woman I have ever known. She had a way with children and we all loved her. She never tried to force her religion on us, she never mentioned it, but I could see how strong and wholesome it was. I don't think she deserved the daughter she got, because my mother was a shrill and demanding shrew if there ever was one, hard and calculating, too. My father (Catholic) was the soul of gentleness and kindness and patience. My heart bled for him. The only times that he ever became firm were when his sisters tried to make good Catholics out of us children (which they were always doing chiefly by the method of denouncing anything and everything that was Jewish). Father *insisted* that we must be allowed to make up our own minds. Make up our own minds, indeed! I was so confused by the sweetness of my father and grandmother and the harshness of Mother and the aunts about everything that the others stood for that I had to grow up, go overseas, and be away from them all for five years before I could get any idea of what I wanted to be, or what life was really all about. Both my brother and sister had much the same experience.

A unified cultural training, it is often said, leads to narrow-mindedness and bigotry in social relationships. Will not a

Catholic, who has been taught Catholicism by his whole family and church, sent to a parochial school, a Catholic college, and kept in a circle of Catholic social relationships, be "intolerant" of the attitudes and behavior of non-Catholics? One wonders, though, about the individual's personality integration. Neuroses come from inner conflicts, that is, from having more than one idea of how to behave, of what to be, of what is right and wrong, of what one believes, and having to choose between them. A child whose parents, school, and church all teach him "the one way," may seem narrow to those of another way, but he has no conflict within himself for he is certain and sure, has no decisions to make, and no pangs of conscience if he follows "the straight and narrow path." For the child, however, whose own parents represent two ways of life, who argue about the right way of living, and who attempt to pull him back and forth between them there is no such certainty. This is quite a burden for a young child to carry. He has no background of experience on which to base a decision. It often happens that such a child cannot make one. He sways back and forth, seeing first the "truth" of what Mother says and then the equal "truth" of what Father says. When they are both good to him and live up to the ideal of each of their religions, it is difficult for him to choose a side. When they are unkind and show evidences of hypocrisy in their faith (which children are very quick to see), the child may become bitter against each religion in turn. Whatever the case may be, he has conflicts about what to do. No matter which way he goes, a haunting pang of conscience follows him for deserting the other way that, after all, is characteristic of one of his own parents. Conflict and guilt feelings are the essence of the neurotic personality; and like the bigoted person, the neurotic is not always successful in his social relationships. These two types may be at opposite ends of a pole, but the child with a unicultural training is at least more comfortable within himself than was the girl in the following case:

> My Mother was a Catholic and my Dad a Protestant. She had been very devout, was the only person in her family who married outside her religion, and she never got over the feeling of guilt about it. Dad didn't go to church himself, but he hated the Catholic religion and he was a stern and domineering man. Mother told us never to mention her religion when his family was around. We kids were *sent*, not taken, to the Methodist church and Sunday school. Often I persuaded my little sisters to play hooky. No one ever knew. It wasn't a very good example for them but I *hate* to be *told* what to do against my will. Later, I fell in love with a Catholic boy. Father was beside himself and insisted upon breaking it up. So . . . we eloped. Dad was right in this one thing, though. My husband was a lazy ne'er-do-well, who ran off four months after we were married. I never got anything out of my marriage except a baby. All of this preyed on Mother's mind so much that she had a breakdown and is in a hospital. Now, I want to have my son christened in the Catholic faith; but Mother isn't here to support me in it, and I know just what would happen with Dad. After my marriage, I don't know whether I should defy Dad, anyway. I just don't seem to know what is right and it's easier just to let things slide.

Some Forms of Intrafamily Arrangements

The manner in which the families in our case records operated in the acculturation of their children is quite varied, but certain general patterns did emerge.

1. A frequent form is the "taking over" of the children by a dominating parent, and silent submission by the other. The results, as voiced by the children, were not too successful. For one thing, one parent always seemed not really to belong to the family. This apparently mattered less if the father was the outsider and the mother was considered a

"good mother" by her children. It was much less satisfactory if those roles were reversed. If the dominating parent was not considered a "good parent," however, sympathy went out to the submissive one, resulting in a break with the family head, and the religion, at the first possible moment.

2. Another pattern shows both parents to be relatively ineffective, or uninterested, in the face of the pressures from their respective kinsfolk. Children feel especially helpless and bitter in such cases. One girl, who lived for periods of time alternately with her father's and mother's people, wrote:

> I went to live with my maternal grandmother . . . and was used as a whipping boy for my uncle to pour out his hatred for the Vatican, the Pope, Archbishops, Bishops, and "scheming" priests of Catholicism. My father's visits there were unwelcome . . . [they] attempted to destroy [my affection for him] by stripping him to ribbons after each of his departures. In the eyes of a small child, it was most cruel, but I clung madly to my belief that my father was a good father. I went to live with my father's people. That side of the house immediately went to work to criticize my upbringing in the family of my mother. They accused them of spoiling me and making me ashamed of my Catholic blood—and inferred we were all born out of wedlock.

3. In some families, when one parent appears to dominate, the other parent is not actually submissive. There is a continuous planned program of subversion for the benefit of the children, though one member of the family is unaware of it. This usually results in children having little respect for either parent when they become fully aware of what has been going on and how one parent has been fooled.

4. There are the cases in which the family is divided by parental prearrangement. "You can have the girls and I'll take the boys," or "You take the first, I'll take the second, and so on." This has its problem aspects, too. First, the chil-

dren do not always agree, and reassort themselves when they are able, with the result in one family that a father forbade his daughter his home when she changed her religion in mid-adolescence, and he did not see nor speak to her for eleven years. Her comment was that he spoke to her again only when he "needed" her. A choice by sexes, then, appears to be dangerously divisive, separating the male and female loyalties and activities into two camps, with a firm line between them. Sex hostility, as well as religious hostility, was marked in a number of these families, and the children remained divided, changing their religions less frequently than in the former pattern.

5. There is a pattern of complete lack of decision. Both the mother and the father fight continuously for all of the children, or for certain of the children. In some cases, even where a plan has been decided upon, the parents change their minds, and this pattern results.

6. Some parents agree to attend to different aspects of their children's lives. One has his say in the religious training; the other, in the educational or social training. There is less conflict in these homes, *provided* the parents mean what they promise, are happy in it and do not interfere with each other, the children agree, and the religious and educational training are not completely incompatible. There is less conflict; but there is no picture of strong family cohesiveness.

7. Finally, there are the parents, usually not practicing members of their own faiths, who take a "hands off" policy, and manage to maintain it. Their children can go to whatever churches they care to or they can go to none; they may attend a "neutral" school, and make their own religious choice. The picture that emerges of children wandering from church to church, trying to find a religious faith, is rather pathetic. Some never can. When they do, they usually

choose because of pleasant social relations rather than because of one set of religious values. If a change in relationships or locale comes about, the search begins all over again. When they are successful, however, their concern usually tends in the direction of their parents, like the little boy, who, finding himself happy in the Friends Meeting, came home one First Day from the service to say, "I wish I had a good Mummy and Daddy like the other kids." Fortunately, in a few of the cases, this attitude in their children had a strong effect upon Mummy and Daddy, and ended with the family uniting religiously, after the children had paid a high price to obtain that end.

In all these forms of intrafamily arrangements, two factors are constant. One is the lack of "certainties" for children to hold onto when family relationships are strained. It is not only interfaith families that have troubles. Many parents are ineffective or dominating. Many marital partners have conflicts, and when they do, the conflicts affect the children and make them uneasy. If their parents are at odds, how can the children be secure, and on whom can they depend? A youngster whose parents were in the process of divorce reported that when she felt most "scared" she found complete assurance in singing her favorite hymn very loudly: "Be not dismayed whate'er betide. God will take care of you." She knew that if she pleased God, as her parents and Sunday school teachers had shown her, everything would turn out all right for her. The child of an interfaith marriage, who is not sure how to please one personal God, lacks this incomparable support to help him carry his problems with confidence. The second constant factor is that, even though the family tensions may spring from the same kind of personality differences that exist in a one-religion family, it is religion that is used as a tool and an epithet. Children not only have no firm religious conviction, but religion has been stressed for them as the cause of their troubles and a divisive influence.

BROTHER-SISTER RELATIONSHIPS

Although most of the books dealing with child development speak of the relationships between brothers and sisters in terms of hostility and jealousy, and how to avoid them, there is some evidence that these relationships may be just as important and constructive as parent-child relationships. If so, some attention to brother-sister interaction is a meaningful part of the story of interfaith families.

The evidences just referred to come from sources of varying degrees of scientific authenticity. In a study of large families, which the authors have made, it was discovered that children thought of their sense of security as coming from their brothers and sisters, the people who were closest to them in age and interests. Even when their parents were bickering or brutal or alcoholic, there were enough children around to present a solid front. Small families do not have this advantage. Yet the father who began early in the life of his two children to stop their quarrels by impressing them with the fact that their family was small, and that they should keep close to each other because the time would come when they had only each other as family, understood the need for family blood ties even after adulthood, marriage, and the establishment of a new family. The third bit of evidence has been suggested in Chapter 6. There is a point in life at which one strikes off the family. It is short lived, and one begins increasingly to take interest in one's roots. The remaining family may then consist of a brother or a sister. It is then that barriers often begin to crumble, and brothers and sisters come closer together again.

It was a very persistent story, in the case records of children of interfaith marriages, that religion had been a barrier between them and one that was difficult to span. Instead of the feelings of the brothers and sisters becoming less hostile with time, the advent of their own children increased awareness of religious differences and made the siblings even more wary of each other and of social communication with each other.

One aspect of early sibling relationships was that the children used religion as a tool in their rivalry with each other for the affections of a preferred parent. There was little that either a mother or father could do to force a particular religion upon a child after a certain age, and especially since one parent was receptive to a change in the child's religion or was actually trying to woo him into it. From this situation came the cases of youngsters weaving back and forth from one religion to another for the sole purpose of gaining favor. Another aspect was that the siblings of one religion used religious epithets for those of the other religion, even in their childhood play, in order to establish superior and inferior statuses. Needless to say, this does not lead to healthy attitudes about any religion, nor to good family relationships. In other cases, the separation was less vocal—in fact, it was nonvocal. There was a firm dividing line as far as religion and observances were concerned. In other areas of family living, they joined together, but the moment religion entered in any way they silently drew apart, as if a wall had suddenly been erected between them. There were instances in which the father and mother did everything in their power to keep one brood of children from "infecting" the other. This was especially marked in one family where it had been decided that the Protestant father would rear all the boys in his faith and the Catholic

mother could do the same with all the girls. When the family
was completed, it was composed of four boys and one girl.
The bargain was kept, but the little girl was reared almost
as if she had no brothers. Her mother, feeling very badly
that she had defied the laws of her church, was determined
to rear her one daughter to be the best possible Catholic, and
would brook no possible anti-Catholic influences from the
Protestant side of the family.

The continuation of this kind of separation in later life
was voiced by a childless married woman of thirty-six: "I
love my nephews and nieces and I need their companionship. There are so many things I could do for them, too. But
my brother is afraid to let us get friendly because of the
differences in our religious beliefs." This sort of situation
occurred, in a slightly different manner, in the following
case:

> I was raised in a small town in Georgia, with my brother who
> was a year younger and my sister two years younger. We were
> a close and happy family, and all the neighbors were like us,
> close, and we all went to the same church. We learned that there
> was one just God and that if we were good He would take care
> of us and make us happy. (This isn't true in mixed marriage. It
> is all bitterness—especially for the future children in that mar-
> riage.) Well, I didn't know that there were other religions than
> mine. I only knew one. That was the only one in our town. We
> lived so happily. Later a handsome young man came from Chi-
> cago to work in our town. He fell in love with me and I was so
> happy because he was so good and fine and so handsome. All the
> other girls envied me. We were married by my minister and I
> hadn't thought anything at all about his religion. We were so in
> love with each other—he loved me deeply, I know. Everything
> was fine, except that I wanted to go to Chicago to meet his folks.
> Something always happened to stop us every time I wanted to
> —he was too busy or he didn't have enough cash, or something.
> Then, I was going to have a baby and was so excited that I for-
> got all about his family for a while. The next thing that happened
> was about the christening of our little boy. Things kept putting

it off, and my husband was getting moody. Finally he told me. He said he was a Jew. I didn't know what difference that made (but it made all the difference, such a terrible difference), and said that we could just have the baby christened and then when we could go to Chicago he could be christened all over again. My husband said no, that would never work, and I thought that this dear, loving man who was so good to me was being very strange. He got more moody and then he told me that he was willing to try it. So the baby was christened, and everything started being all right again. We were a happy family until the next baby came. She was a little girl. Now my husband became not like himself at all. He said he had let the boy be christened against his religion and that he just had to take the girl to Chicago. That was all right with me. I would get to know his family at last.

We left the boy with my folks and went to see his family. Then I found it all out. On the way to Chicago he told me that we had left the boy because his family could not have anything to do with him. They couldn't with me until I went through a "cleansing." I said he was so dear and fine that his family would be just like him and when we got there everything would clear up. I didn't know. When I got there I saw how different Jews are, and he got just like them while he was home. They put me through the "cleansing" and I got so sick I couldn't even take care of the baby, and by the time I got well enough to go home again she was a Jew. Back home nobody knew anything about all this. They still were all jealous of my fine husband and my babies—but now I was jealous of them. Little did they know!

Then, our family was happy again. It was the same as before. We loved each other and our babies very much, and he was a good and loving father to them. When it was time for our boy to go to college we sent him to one near to home. The girl had to be sent to his family's to live and go to college there.

Four years she lived there and fell in love with a Jewish boy and married him. I felt so sick. I thought I would hardly ever see her again, and I thought now she is going to have all the heartache that I had. What have I done to her? She was happy though, just like I had been, and things seemed to work out all right. She had a little baby girl. My husband told me I ought to go out and visit with her. By now her girl was 7. Everything seemed so nice. She had a nice home and fine things and husband and

little girl. Then she told me, "Mother, what did you do to me?
I am not a Jew and I never will be one. I want to go back home
where I was so happy. My little girl is playing with Jewish
children and when she grows up and gets married where will this
stop? Does it have to be heartache after heartache? Why did
you separate me from my brother? Why couldn't I go to the
college he went to? This is an awful thing to lose my brother
and never to have my little girl know my brother's children."

I went back home sadder than ever, because I knew that all the
things that happened to me were things she had, too. My brother
and sister found out about everything, too. They were nice and
kind to me, but they didn't want their babies to get near to my
husband and they never could know my little girl's baby.

To Whom Do I Belong?

Human beings seem to have a need to be accepted completely and as they are, without pretenses or defenses, by
other human beings. It is not enough to be loved partially,
so that one has to pretend something or hide something in
order to be accepted. That is a great effort and a nervous
strain. For peace of mind and body, it is necessary to have
someone with whom one can relax and be one's self. The
most obvious source of such relaxation and acceptance is
the members of the family. The many children who go
through "adoption fantasy" show the truth of this. They
have somehow gotten a notion that their parents love them
only partially, that there is something about them that their
parents do not accept. So, they decide that they do not
really belong to those parents, but have been adopted; and
they press their parents hard. These children want assurance
that, no matter what they are, their family likes them that
way, or that there is another family that will. This feeling
extends beyond childhood, however, as witnessed by many
mature (and unhappy) people who actually have been

adopted and who spend much effort and time to trace their own origins.

Children of interfaith marriages, in cases where the parents cannot come to full and sincere agreement about their rearing, have to cope with the problem of total acceptance. They know full well that there is something about them that one or both parents do not like. Here is one illustration of the development of such knowledge in a five-year-old boy. His mother, a Gentile, married a Jewish man, with the agreement that any children would be reared in her faith. The agreement was kept, and for the first five years of his life the boy knew only the maternal side of the family. Then he was introduced to his father's family. Several "incidents" occurred. First, a member of his father's family commented that the lad certainly was a real Cohen. Whereupon the boy denied this rather violently and identified himself with his mother's family. The Cohens reacted just as could be expected, and the boy drank in those reactions. A short time afterward, he innocently remarked that the corned beef was the best ham he had ever tasted. This time there was a deafening silence, which the child also noted. Later he asked his mother why they were so different from Aunt So-and-So. She tried to explain to him. At the end of the explanation, he asked: "Mummy, to whom do I really belong?" His mother felt sure that, in spite of the crises he had precipitated in his father's family, he would not have asked such a question had he been sure that she loved him exactly as he was. She did love him very much, but she was worried about the shape of his nose. She just did not like it, nor did she like the way in which he was beginning to pronounce words the way his father did—a far cry from her own southern accent.

Human beings not only need to be accepted as they are,

but to be so accepted by someone whom they respect. It is of little value to be loved by anyone else. In the cases where children loved both the mother and the father equally, and yet had to deal with a religious difference between them and their families, the burden was heavy and bitter. To whom should he belong? It might be decided for him for a while, but eventually he had to make his own choice. He could decide on one or the other, or neither. Here is the story of one man:

> There was never a time in my life when I first became conscious of religion. Like the concept of "mother," it seemed always to have been present as a great and awful question upon which adults did not agree, and upon which they would brook no discussion.
>
> One of the most perplexing experiences of my early childhood was the peculiarity of church attendance. My father always went to church on Sunday morning, and usually took me along. Occasionally, mother went with him, although frequently she stayed at home. Then, in the afternoon, my grandmother and uncle (maternal) took me to another church. The difference between the two services was quite apparent but incomprehensible to me, since questions were entirely taboo. In time I came to know that Father was a Catholic, Grandmother was Presbyterian, and Mother was a "backslider." This was all very confusing and beyond my powers of comprehension, but the "backslider" seemed to be the most desirable church as it did not require attendance.
>
> At the Catholic church I was taught that to miss Mass was a sin. If so, I questioned, why didn't Mother go to Mass or why did Uncle Charley go to the wrong church. Not being able to get any satisfaction from my folks, I once asked the Sunday school teacher. She told me something about "old time religion" and "Papish pageantry." The words stuck, but all that it seemed to mean was that Father's church was wrong, and that he had done something very bad to Mother.
>
> When I was about three years of age I remember much hushed conversation which took place among Mother, Father,

Grandmother, Uncle Charley, and several other people. They all talked for a long time behind closed doors; then, when they came out, they all kissed me. Mother cried when Grandmother and Uncle Charley left, and they did not visit us again for a long time. From this time on, Mother went to Mass regularly, since she had become a Catholic.

Then Grandmother's father died. He seemed to be a very old man, and since we all went to the funeral, this was a very happy occasion for me as it brought all the family together again. What I didn't understand was that both families were very proud of their religious heritage although both were more inclined to lip service than to devotion.

My father was of the second generation from a central and northern European family of petty nobility. It had tenaciously remained Catholic until Bismarck's time, when it migrated to America as the solution to what seemed an intolerable situation abroad. Father, by his very marriage with a Protestant, had greatly weakened the hold of an isolated, sacred, patriarchal family. He had been gradually breaking with his religion, which was more of a political tradition of the family than a belief in or worship of God, and as the family ties disintegrated the Church lost most of its significance. For a time he became a Modernist; then, when in 1907 Pope Pius X condemned modernism as subversive of ecclesiastical authority and Father could no longer remain a member of the Church in good standing, reconciling dogma and biblical teaching with modern science and philosophy, he ceased to attend church altogether, and proclaimed himself an agnostic.

Mother was a descendant of Dutch Huguenots and English Friends who had migrated to America in the early seventeenth century. They had been highly successful in this country, and pointed with much pride to members of the family who had become Governors and Divines even before the Revolutionary War. During all of this time they had tenaciously upheld the tradition of America for Americans, which, of course, meant Protestants who could point to ancestry from western Europe.

The two families never mingled. I visited Father's people with him; they never visited us. I did not know many of Mother's folks, since they also avoided us. Those whom I came to know, I met through Grandmother or Uncle Charley. This lack of relatives and family spirit, so common among many of my friends, annoyed me greatly, but when I asked about it the answer was always evasive.

When I became old enough for school a long debate resulted. Finally, it was agreed that I should attend parochial school until I had received the sacraments, then I was to be sent to the public or possibly to a private Friends' school.

After about two years in the parochial school, Father became very incensed at some of what he called the "superstitious nonsense" they were teaching and insisted that I be sent to the public school. This was one of the few occasions on which I heard Father speak severely, and the second occasion on which I had seen Mother cry. During the remainder of my precollegiate education, I was frequently shifted from one school to another, and I began to understand the reason.

Mother, whose nature was poetic, bordering upon superstitious, found peace, assurance, security, and beauty in the Catholic church, which contrasted so greatly with the cold, Calvinistic doctrines of her puritanical ancestors. Hers was a religion of joy. She prayed much, doubted nothing, and never for a moment questioned salvation through Jesus. She simply added the sacraments, belief in good works, and emotional formalism to make the guarantee of future happiness more certain. Father, a scientist who never had much faith of any sort and was now freed from his family's domination, emerged an agnostic after years of professing Christianity in which he did not believe.

During my early years, the only problem which ever concerned me to which I couldn't obtain an answer was that of religion. I loved my father and my mother, who seemed always to agree on everything but this one subject. I was taught that God was just, holy, and merciful, yet, according to Grandmother, it was wrong to play cards or read a paper or even study on Sunday. Father taught me to go to Mass, but as I grew older, he didn't do it himself, and Mother, who had been a Protestant and who, at one time, had not gone to any church, now insisted that I go to Mass.

By the time I entered college, I was horribly confused. First, I went to one church, then to another; finally, I stopped going altogether. The only thing in life that seemed uncertain was religion, or, now, God. I had just about emancipated myself from all religions when I fell in love with a Catholic girl, and married her as a Catholic.

This has simply renewed the problem that confronted my parents. When I married, I promised to live as Catholic and raise any children in that faith. For a while I blindly did as I had promised, but as time went on I could not continue. I am as agnostic as my father. I also must make religious discussions taboo and realize that a deep and abysmal chasm separates my wife and myself from what might otherwise be an ideal partnership. Fortunately, we have no children, and will not have any, and we manage to bridge the gulf by silence on the topic.

Personally, I'm against any religious differences in marriage.

The Children's Friendships

Apparently some of the difficulties of the marital partners of a mixed marriage in forming friendships become a part of the inheritance of the younger generation. Our records show several problems in this respect, some of them caused by the family and others by the friends. They will be mentioned only briefly, to avoid repetition.

First, children when very young are not aware of social distinctions such as religions unless adults make the children aware. They like some children just because they like them, and dislike others because they do not. A family that is religiously divided, however, is very conscious of differences in faith because they are highlights in their lives, and their children realize there are these differences before they are old enough to understand them. As one girl, with very keen insight, commented: "Families who have had children marry outside their religion have the same reaction to one thing, I have noticed. Upon discussing or upon meeting someone new, the first question asked about said person is his religion. It suddenly seems quite important to them, even to those members of the family who only attend church once a year. Religion becomes the issue of issues." Something that started early in the lives of children in our records was the family's sizing up of playmates on the basis of their faiths, and this kept up even more emphatically during adolescence, when children's loyalties to their friends are so strong. For instance:

> In my friendships I find my mother's people accepting readily my Protestant friends and defending them if I do any fault finding. However, my Catholic friends never reach the sanctum sanctorum of my family. They are always politely received, little is said about them or to them and there is never an invitation for them to return. I am generally cautious when I invite my Catholic friends for the reaction to such an invitation is one of general annoyance when they are discussed and not too complimentary remarks are made following their departure. When the friends are Protestant they are immediately accepted and after their departure they most always say, "Jane . . . well, now, there's a fine girl! Why don't you bring more like her home?" This entire difficulty became so disturbing to me that, in order to keep my friends, I moved to a small apartment of my own as soon as I was able, where I entertain anyone I choose to.

In a few families where the house was firmly divided against itself, the children of one faith were permitted one set of friends and the children of the other faith, another set. It need scarcely be described how unsatisfactory this was in terms both of friendships and of sibling relationships.

The deepest problem of all, in friendships, may be illustrated by the experience of an attractive young girl of nineteen who came weeping bitterly to talk over her problem. Her mother was Jewish and her father Gentile. She looked like her father, and bore his name. When she fell in love with a Gentile boy, she did not mention her mixed parentage. Shortly before they were to be married, he discovered it through rumor, questioned her, and was given the truth. Abruptly the engagement was terminated.

THE FAMILY THROUGH THE YEARS

Just as marriages age, change, and meet with crises, so do families. Perhaps it will prove helpful in this connection to speak of the family cycle, which many students of the family have emphasized in recent years. The idea is that family histories consist of a series of stages, each of which presents its own interests, activities, tensions, and problems. Some writers speak of the founding, the expanding, and the contracting stages of a family. Others elaborate the central idea in greater detail, speaking of (a) the marriage stage, where the emphasis is mostly upon relations between husband and wife; (b) the child-bearing stage, covering the years from the coming of the first to the last birth; (c) the years preoccupied with problems of child rearing and education; (d) the child-launching stage, with occupational and/or social aspects; (e) the stage where the children are courting and marrying; and finally (f) the stage of the empty nest, when father and mother are thrown upon each other, to await the grandparent stage. Many families, of course, do not conform to these stages. Some of them go through three stages at one time. Others are completely unclassifiable by these categories, but are just as significant in themselves.

Each stage in the cycle is characterized by its own specific problems for the parents and children in a mixed religious family. In the earliest stages the difficulties may be minor, for man and wife are concerned first with themselves and then with the physical care and habit training of babies—and not very much with the babies' ideas. It is later that uncertainties about education and relations outside the family arise; still later that the sorts of young people with whom children date, court, and marry come into focus; and even later when the married couple find themselves alone again, deprived of the children who were their chief common interest, faced with beginning together again pretty much as they did when they were first married, and wondering just how their grandchildren are going to be reared. The fact is that such families do not ordinarily face and solve once and for all, early in life, the decisions necessitated by their kind of marriage. New ones arise throughout the whole cycle of family life to disturb and create a need for readjustments.

THE CHILDREN'S DECISIONS

Quite apart from parents' intentions for children and the pressures upon them as they grow up, the children ultimately decide for themselves. Many studies of the second generation in these families state what happens. Children keep to the religion in which they were reared; they choose the religion of one parent or the other; they choose a "neutral" church; or they become nonpracticing or agnostics or atheists.

A very careful analysis of our data suggests that all these ways are taken, but that this is too simple a story. The very great majority of the children never did make one certain decision to which they clung throughout life. They turned *from*, they turned *back*, they tried another, they gave it up. This was the general pattern, but in endless variations. Of these variations, the major portion ended, at the date of recording, with "nonpracticing." Many indicated that they were not happy about this decision, but had been unable to find a church in which they felt comfortable.

A part of their decision about religion was evidenced by their marriages. It is widely accepted as fact that children of mixed marriages themselves mix-marry more frequently than do children from one-faith families. Our analysis showed clearly that the majority of the children did marry outside of the faith in which they had been reared. Where our records included a third generation, definite patterns again emerged. About half of the second-generation parents who had turned from their faith and married outside of it let their spouses take over the religious training of the children. The other half made strong attempts to turn their children back to the religion of their own childhood. This was sometimes successful, and sometimes it was not.

The accompanying chart is the best illustration available to us of a family religious-life history through four generations, to the birth of the first child of the fifth generation. It tells its own story of religious choice, marital selection, and the religious training of youngsters in the lives of people who were the products of an interfaith marriage.

RELIGION TODAY

This chart of a four-generation family may lead to a question which is very common among a number of people at the present time. What about Ruth, the first member of the fifth generation? Since Joseph and Marguerite, her great-great-grandfather and great-great-grandmother were married, the world has changed a great deal. Religion was then a stronger force. Life has become increasingly secularized and tolerant. Will not Ruth be able to make an interfaith marriage without the social stigma and inner conflict that her predecessors encountered? Perhaps so, if she has become completely secular and completely tolerant. It is very risky, however, to assume that Ruth will be like this just because of the past secular and individualistic trend, and it is risky for several reasons. The first one has already been suggested —that people rarely escape fully from their past cultural heritage even when they temporarily believe that they have.

The second reason has to do with a recent and noticeable revival of religious feeling in our country and among young people. It has not happened to all of them, of course. Some

AN INTERFAITH FAMILY THROUGH FOUR GENERATIONS TO THE FIFTH

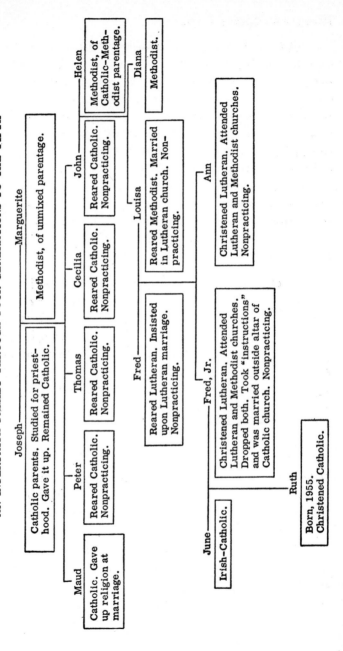

are more secular than their parents. Others, however, are not, and many of these are youngsters who have felt deprived of a very important part of life by parents who would not or could not give it to them. During a recent conference on family relations at which young people were invited to take part and ask questions of "family experts," one of the authors who was present noted with what glib facility these "experts" answered all the young people's questions, except one. A teen-aged girl arose and stated that the problem which worried her and her friends most was that so many of their parents were agnostics. What could the children do about that? A deadly silence fell on the conference. Finally, the moderator had to pass the meeting on to another question. This seemed very much like a signpost pointing to the quest of a younger generation being ignored and unaided by a former, more secular generation.

Many aspects of life seem to fluctuate in cycles. Children from a large family usually want smaller families when they marry; those from small families want to have more children. It may take a long time for these patterns actually to crystallize as a societal habit. The family has been small, in reaction to a larger one, during the whole present century; but indications are that it is now growing larger again. In similar vein, it has been quite noticeable to the authors who have worked with hundreds of young people that many children of the hardest drinking, chain-smoking parents tend to react by being much more moderate in these things than their parents. The revival of religious feeling may be a part of the same tendency.

Since these cycles start through the behavior of scattered individuals and gradually gain momentum and favor before they become a new social pattern—if they do—we may now be living through a time of especially great distress for the children who are the pioneers of the reaction. It is very easy for the secularized young couple of today to reason that their marriage will be no problem to their child because religion is unimportant to them. It is, however, quite impossible for them to know what will be their child's attitude toward religion. For generations past, parents have been presented with the anguish of seeing their children depart from religion. This feeling is well understood and it creates sympathy for the parents. Perhaps a new kind of anguish, less understood, is coming to be that of watching a child turn away from his secular parents to resolve his conflicts and find comfort in religion. These parents may need greater sympathy than the former ones because they will very likely have deeper feelings of inadequacy, guilt, and possibly, inferiority to their own children.

In this chapter it has been pointed out that people who make interfaith marriages apparently realize that children will cause problems or will have problems. The lower birth rate and higher rate of childlessness among such couples suggest this. A part of the difficulty is caused by a primary function of the family—to pass down the cultural heritage. When the parents are of different religions, the family is a cultural mixture and the child is torn, in choosing his religion and philosophy of life, between two sides of the family. This results not only in "taking sides" within the family, but in inner conflict for the child. The divisiveness extends to brothers and sisters as well as to parents and tends to separate them even when they grow up, marry, and have their own children who are reared in various faiths. Children of an interfaith marriage find some of the same problems in making friends that their parents had, with the additional difficulty of having their parents bicker about which friends are suitable. Apparently, all of this causes a certain amount of restlessness, for many of the cases under study never could choose a religion once and for all. They changed back and forth and most of them ended by being nonpracticing. Because of the recent revival of religious feeling among young people, the parents' nonpracticing status may become an added problem to them if their children reject their parents' secularism and turn again to religion for comfort and direction.

CHAPTER EIGHT

Solutions That Have Worked

Every marriage, like life itself, consists of a series of problems and crises. When people say they have had no problems in their married life, what they mean is that theirs have been minor in degree or that they have met them successfully. Mixed marriages present their own distinctive kinds of problems, in addition to those which characterize other marriages. The preceding pages have attempted to show the nature and variety of these.

Are these problems insoluble? Are persons who cross the religious line, especially when it separates widely different religious cultures, inevitably doomed to conflict, unhappiness, and often the ultimate dissolution of divorce? Are there any ways out? What can one do to salvage such marriages, or to build them wisely from the start? How do people who make such marriages manage? What patterns of adjustment do we find? These are matters which we wish to discuss in this final chapter.

151

TYPES OF AMERICAN REACTION TO PROBLEMS

Living with a problem has not been favored much as a policy in the American way of life and thought. We Americans tend to be impatient and restive with problems. We have none of the resigned acceptance of fate such as finds expression among Sicilians in their philosophy of "e tu destino" or the meditative submission of traditional oriental groups.

This impatience tends to express itself in several ways. One of these has been the American habit of running away from problems. To say this is to startle some readers and to call forth indignant denial from them. Yet, so penetrating an analyst of American life as the late James Truslow Adams spoke of this as a characteristic American trait. This country, he pointed out, was settled by successive waves of immigrants who ran away from their problems at home and came to this country to escape them. Later this process was repeated on a large scale in the westward march of population, with successive waves of people leaving the older, settled areas, with their problems, for the "green grass" of newer opportunities. More recently, the exodus of city families to the suburbs, and from the suburbs to the areas between the radial lines of transportation, can be given a similar interpretation. Obviously, other meanings have been advanced for these population movements, and with good reason, but Mr. Adams' indictment cannot be wholly ignored.

A second way in which American impatience with problems expresses itself is in our confident expectation of miracle cures for all kinds of problems. One might call this the penicillin attitude. Is someone seriously ill? Give him a few doses of the latest wonder drug and let him be on his way.

Is there an unconquered disease? Catch five scientists, give them six million dollars, lock them in a laboratory for a year, and lo, another wonder drug. Is there a social problem? Call an expert, and direct him: "Pray, sir, it is now four o'clock. Please tell us how we can do away with this evil so that we may catch the 5:15 train for home." So with mixed marriages. "Dear authors, we wish to make them. Please tell us how we can do this without any of the attendant problems." All this is not meant to be facetious or sarcastic, but rather to express concretely the philosophy of the American mind concerning problems, and its conception of the magic wonders of science. Since science has performed miracles with atoms, robots, dacron, and air conditioning, why not with the marriage of an Orthodox Jewish rabbi and a devout Catholic!

A third expression of the American attitude toward problems is to order them to go away. This is often called the "ordering-and-forbidding technique" of solving problems. That is to say, the problem is ordered to go away, by eloquent words or legal phrases or inspired pleas. We say people ought to do thus and so, and that if they will follow these directions, presto, their problems will be solved. And it would be pleasant to write the rest of this chapter in that way, for it would permit us to give voice to some very pious platitudes, and these might be pleasing to some of our readers. Many books on human problems end in this way, and it has its compensations. It gives authors a feeling of achievement and readers a sense of assurance.

Happily or unhappily, as the reader will choose, this is not the plan followed here. We shall present realistic forms of adjustment which we have found in our many years of study of mixed marriages. If this lacks the fervor of social evangelism, it has at least the merit of concrete reality.

PATTERNS OF ADJUSTMENT

The patterns of adjustment which we present, and the illustrative cases, are those in which *both* parties to the marriage give reasonable evidence of happiness and satisfaction. This is an important distinction because some of the persons who make mixed marriages and speak of them as successful are actually speaking only for themselves.

We shall illustrate this with the experience of persons who handle child-adoption cases. Over and again, married couples come to some agency and ask for a child for adoption. Early in the proceedings, it will be noticed that one of the couple does all of the talking. Subsequent investigation often shows that the other member really is lukewarm, indifferent, skeptical, or even antagonistic to the idea. We have found the same situation in the case of mixed marriages. One of the married pair is loud in defense or praise of mixed marriages in general and his own in particular, when our fuller information shows the other one to have different, and often widely differing, feelings. An air of resignation may be interpreted by an eager mate as willing acceptance on the part of the other, when actually it covers a smoldering resentment.

There is the choice story, for instance, of the English woman who was an eager advocate of international marriages as a solution to the world's problems. In accordance with her own beliefs, she married a Mexican. Later on, in speaking of her own marriage and how happy it had all been, she mentioned their lovely apartment *in London*, and the fact that *once a week* she even prepared Mexican dishes for her husband. The husband's statement about the marriage could not be obtained..

We have not meant to imply that such marriages are

completely unhappy, even when one mate does not agree with the other in regard to the problems and adjustments resulting from their mixed marriage. In many, perhaps all, marriages there are areas of disagreement between the couple. This is aptly documented in a study by Judson Landis of 409 couples, married on an average of twenty years, and identified as having made successful marriages. Six areas of married life were covered. These were sex relations, spending family income, social activities, in-law relationships, religious activities, and mutual friends. Landis found that the percentages of couples who never worked out a satisfactory adjustment varied from 7.9 for mutual friends to 12.5 for sex relations to 13.8 for social and recreational activities. Approximately 10 per cent of the husbands and wives failed to reach a satisfactory adjustment in each of the six areas. What is particularly significant in this connection is that husbands and wives often disagreed as to whether adjustment had been made. Where disagreement occurred, the husbands more frequently than the wives believed that the adjustment had been satisfactory.

It is clear, therefore, that a lack of appreciation by one mate of the other mate's dissatisfaction with some facet of their married life is common, and not confined to the area of religious differences. From what has been said in an earlier chapter about the real nature of interfaith differences, it should be equally clear that this might well be an area peculiarly prone to involve such misunderstandings.

Proceeding now to the type patterns of adjustment apparently acceptable to mixed marriages, we shall present six, each with illustrations which, it is hoped, will clarify the essential elements involved.

1. One of the situations in which we have found mixed marriages to work out successfully is where one of the

mates accepts the religious culture of the other. Two case histories are presented where this has happened with apparent success.

James Donovan was an Irish lad, one of eleven children, who grew up in a poor family, living in a stranded area where life bore down heavily on most of its people. His early life was unhappy, and the Catholic priest in his parish was said to be unhealthy, unhappy, and unsympathetic toward his young people. At the age of twenty, James was given the opportunity by a Protestant friend to go to a Protestant college, where, by dint of this outside aid, part-time employment, and earnest application, he was graduated with a fine record. In his second year at college he met an attractive girl, soloist in the Methodist church, a Methodist herself, and the daughter of a father with fine intellectual interests. James was attracted to the father as well as to his daughter. As the courtship progressed, he attended the Methodist church regularly and spent much time with the girl's family. Shortly before his graduation from college, he joined the Methodist church. The change apparently was sincere, and has remained permanent. The marriage has been a happy one for more than a quarter of a century, and there are two children, both Methodist-reared. James has broken with his past, partially with his family, completely with his first church. He has chosen the way of religious life and thought of his wife, and has had no apparent regrets.

Sylvia was one of the most attractive girls in high school. She had an unmistakable Jewish name, of which she was ashamed, for as she grew up she rejected more and more her Orthodox parents, her Old World grandparents, the attentions of Jewish boys, and the friendships of Jewish girls. One night, at a school dance, she danced with Johnny McFadden, a popular Irish boy. Some years later, she told how that night, before going to sleep, she said aloud over and over again the words "Sylvia McFadden." Ten months after their initial dance, she became Sylvia McFadden. She took instruction in the Catholic faith, she joined John's church, she became an active Catholic. As the years went by, she seemed to become more of a Catholic than her husband. Their children have been reared as Catholics.

The particular religions involved in these two cases are incidental. The important facts are the patterns of adjustment they represent. Both are instances of the acceptance of the religious culture of the one mate by the other. Moreover, the two cases possibly illustrate two different ways or degrees with which this may be done. In the first case, James Donovan's acceptance of his wife's church was apparently the result of sincere conviction, intellectual as well as emotional. In the case of Sylvia, her acceptance of Catholicism may have resulted from her eagerness to escape from a Judaism she had already rejected.

Adjustments of the kind described in these two cases tend to raise certain questions. How sincere and permanent are the conversions of James Donovan and of Sylvia in the two cases just described? What problems of relationship to kinsfolk are raised by the conversion of these two? Are they withdrawing entirely from the families in which they were reared and the people who are their own blood kin? Finally, what does it do to the conceptions of James and Sylvia of their own selves, thus to reject one's past, one's family, one's background? It might even be asked, what does James Donovan's wife and Sylvia McFadden's husband think of their respective mates' self-effacement, as it were?

One need not be an expert in the study of human nature to see questions of this kind arise inevitably.

2. A solution to the problems of a mixed marriage may be found in relative social isolation, that is, a withdrawal from most social contacts by the couple involved.

Richard and Dinah were such a couple. He was a member of one of the more formal, ritualistic Protestant churches. She belonged to a sect known as the "Holy Rollers." Their marriage not only combined two widely differing religions but was also a crossing of the social-class line. He came from the right side of the railroad tracks; she, from the other side. Their marriage occasioned much comment and many forecasts of the "I'll give them six months" variety. The prevailing judgment was that the attraction between them was wholly sexual; and when, six months after the wedding, a baby was born, it was generally agreed that was "the way she got him." This marriage has now lasted more than fifteen years. Almost immediately after the wedding, they located in a relatively isolated spot, more than twelve miles from the city where both had lived. He goes to work in the city regularly, spends his days there, maintaining contact with his male friends at his club, and returns home at night. She has busied herself with their children, and entertains her "Holy Roller" women friends on an occasional afternoon. Both have become enthusiastic gardeners. During the winter months, he spends his "at home" time doing carpentry work on their home. Some of his friends say that his urbanity is a cloak for an unhappy heart, and that both are too stubborn to admit a mistake which both must realize has been made. But their marriage gives every outward appearance of being successful, and the physical appearance of both belies any gnawing secret unhappiness. Perhaps the final test of this marriage will come as the children grow older, and decisions, particularly social ones, must be made.

It is not unreasonable to believe that whatever success this marriage has had has been aided by the relative social isolation of their home life. By the device of putting space between themselves and their acquaintances, they have insulated their home life against the hurts and invidious comparisons that otherwise might have worked against them. Many interracial unions find isolation as their solution.

3. Another way out, identified by some students of the family, is spoken of as personal schematization. This is merely a high-sounding way of saying "You go your way and I'll go mine."

Dan and Polly worked it out this way. Dan was a Baptist, partly by persuasion, largely by family heritage. He was a quiet, patient man, industrious—and stubborn. He loved Polly, who was a Roman Catholic, but not for a dozen Pollys would he budge one bit from being a Baptist. Polly knew her own mind, too, and that mind was to be a good Catholic, to go to mass and confession regularly, to contribute to the church, and to respect the priest. And so it remained. Dan went to the Baptist church occasionally, most often by himself. Polly went to mass regularly, always by herself. Dan thought that Catholicism was kind of silly, as were its living requirements, but if that was what Polly wanted, well, let her have it. Polly thought Dan was a stubborn old dodo, unfortunate in "being brought up so silly," but he was a satisfactory husband, a steady worker, and a good provider. On the subject of planned parenthood, Dan stood firm. Since he would have to support the children, he would assume the responsibility for their coming, and if this was a sin, well, it was his, not Polly's. Polly protested, but if that was the way Dan wanted it, well, the sin *was* his.

Their marriage was a valid one, Dan having given the necessary guarantees. But the longer he thought about it, the less inclined he was to have the children reared as Catholics. Especially was he unwilling if there should be sons. Ultimately what happened was a following of the common European practice with children in case of a mixed marriage. The son was brought up as a Baptist; the daughter, as a Roman Catholic.

Friends of this couple agree that it has been the balanced personalities and the sense of humor of Dan and Polly that have enabled them to find a relatively acceptable solution for the past fourteen years. The differences in the religious rearing of the two children will have its own meaning for the children through all the years of their relationship.

4. Some couples, not many to be sure, find a solution in an agreement that there shall be no children in their families. The effectiveness of certain contraceptives now in use is such that sophisticated couples feel relatively secure in making such an agreement.

Mary, a Roman Catholic, and Morris, a Reformed Jew, contracted an invalid marriage. Mary was the oldest of thirteen children. As often happens in such situations, she was called upon to be a second mother to the brood of younger children. The family had been very poor. Two brothers were killed during World War II, another one was lamed in a motorcycle accident. Her father had been in ill-health for years and had worked only intermittently. As she became older, she rebelled against her fate, her exploitation by her family, her Catholicism which she blamed for its size, and life in general for the series of petty misfortunes that weighed her down. By the time she was twenty-two, she became rather indifferent about her church obligations, going to church only a few times a year.

Morris had been an earnest Jew in his earlier years, but the persecution of Jews during the Hitler days made him decide that when he married he would not bring any more Jews into this hostile world. In many ways, he felt toward his religion the same numb indifference that Mary felt toward hers. As their courtship progressed, they shared their misgivings about life; in fact, encouraged each other's attitude. The invalid marriage, the resolve to have no children, both fell into place in their common attitude.

In the years that followed, neither broke completely with his religious past, but neither was sufficiently involved to create any problems for their relations with each other. One cannot say that Mary and Morris were completely happy. The most that can be said is that their marriage was a negative success, and that whatever tensions arose in its course were never due to any conflict between their Judaism and Catholicism. After some twelve years of life together, Mary spoke at times about the absence of children of her own, but the matter never passed the talking stage. Life has borne down heavily on these two, and their common experience has united them in a certain numbness, as it were, of which childlessness often is the result, mixed marriage or no.

5. This book would not be complete without recognizing that many people today are somewhat less than sympathetic in their attitude toward religion and the church. These attitudes vary from casual indifference to open antagonism. In some cases, such persons reveal well-organized personalities who have found the satisfactions which religion gives to others in their devotion to various causes and ideologies; in many cases, the revolt against religion is only a phase of a

larger situation which finds these persons culturally foot-
loose, with values, philosophies, and life objectives confused
and unstable. Some of these are young men and women passing through the preadult stages of rebellion; some are middle
aged, still seeking for answers; still others are older, cynical,
disillusionized, hard, and perhaps bitter. Each of these shades
of reaction toward religion and/or the church has its meaning in connection with the problems discussed in this volume, but when persons in this group mate with each other,
whatever their traditional religious differences may be, they
have this common bond of indifference to the church and
what it stands for. Harry and Esther were such a pair.

Harry was twenty-three when he met Esther. He had
just secured his Master's degree at a reputable university and
was planning to go on to work for the doctorate. His was
a critical, inquiring type of mind, which found keen satisfaction in his devotion to scientific work. Although a Protestant by family heritage, he thought of himself as a scientist
in distinction to being a religionist, and prided himself on
being tough minded. To him, life was a test tube, a laboratory, a field for scientific analysis and management. Differences between people, like race and religion, were superficial, having meaning only for persons who were prejudiced
and narrow minded. He spoke often of the "herd" mind.
He himself was a scientist, guided by fact and intelligence,
and rose above these human pettinesses.

Esther was an intellectually stimulated Jewess, a brilliant
student, with a tremendous drive for achievement and success. Her Judaistic heritage was not a thing to be proud of,
to cherish and pass on, but a hindrance in forging ahead.
Moreover, its ritualistic features struck her as silly, and she
shuddered whenever she saw her old grandfather with his

long beard. Esther saw her future in terms of high honors in education; a successful marriage with a like-minded intellectual, preferably a non-Jew with an English-sounding name; a home in the suburbs, eventually with two children and two cars; and status in a socially acceptable circle of friends.

Harry and Esther were married on the basis of their common interests and ambitions. The ceremony was performed in the office of a civil official. After their marriage, they went to no church, and their two children have not gone to Sunday school or church. The family life was organized on the basis of intellectual pursuits; the code of conduct emphasized was constructed in terms of intellectual judgments; and the satisfactions of life were derived from material success as a byproduct of scientific achievement. After fourteen years of married life, Harry and Esther cannot see the slightest objection to a mixed marriage. They point to their own happiness; they are self-sufficient, they insist, having cut themselves off entirely from their respective families. And as for success—"Well, look at our home, our cars, our children. Mixed marriage problems? Whatever are you folks talking about?"

6. Finally, there is the solution of compromise between intelligent persons who both give and take on the issues involved in a mixed marriage. This is the answer which the intellectual experts tend to make to the problems of such marriages. Their line of thought is somewhat as follows. Every marriage brings together people who differ in some respects in the backgrounds from which they come. Mixed marriages differ from other marriages not so much in kind as in degree. Interference from the families of the mixed pair, trouble made by their respective friends, issues inherent

in the basic conflict between the two religions, these are serious. But if the couple understands all these complications and difficulties, if their love is strong enough, if their personalities are balanced enough, and if they are sufficiently intelligent, then it may be possible to work out everything happily. In fact, the very strength of character developed under these combined stresses, and the different traditions and values brought together, may enrich the family life of such couples.

There are, of course, some very big ifs in the foregoing paragraph. And couples where both have the necessary poise and intelligence are not always easy to find. Perhaps this particular pattern of adjustment may have more appeal for upper-middle-class intellectuals than for any other element in the population. Arthur and Edith are such a couple.

Arthur is a Roman Catholic. He is a very well-educated man, especially along classical lines, and practices in an honored profession. He is reckoned a successful man, and is universally respected by his associates for his abilities, his judgment, and his sense of fair play. At the age of thirty-one, he married Edith, a Protestant, stemming from a long line of Protestants of a well-known denomination. Edith is intelligent, well-bred, and known among her friends as a well-poised and cultured woman. She was twenty-nine when she married Arthur.

The case of Arthur and Edith is a particularly interesting one because their backgrounds and interests are very similar, save for the differences in their religious rearing. No class nor other cultural distinctions exist to complicate the problem of their marriage. Moreover, they both have reached an age of maturity such as is frequently lacking in marriages of this kind.

At the present writing, they have been married for more than a third of a century. They agree that they have been happy, and all who know them have the same opinion. They frankly admit that there were "hurdles" earlier in their married life, and some continuing disagreements, but that patience and respect for each other have enabled them to work things out. Edith has often said that it would be a mistake to assume that a Protestant-Catholic marriage does not present some very real problems, but she is equally insistent that there are ways out if the couple tries, and respect each other.

There are three children in this family. All three have been reared as Catholics. Edith did not find it easy to do this, especially with the oldest child, who is a daughter in her own image. But, having promised to do so at the time of her marriage, she kept her promise. Arthur, for his part, accepted contraceptives in the spacing of children. Since Edith was twenty-nine at the time of her marriage, and Arthur was thirty-one, both of them agreed on the intelligence of contraceptive usage.

In regard to their social life, Arthur has mingled mostly with his professional associates, without reference to their religious persuasion; Edith has looked after all their other social activities, again without regard to religious selection. Their friends are mostly upper-middle-class professional persons, and religion does not seem to "figure" in their social life.

In presenting this case, the authors have no question about the happiness of Arthur and Edith. Being the kind of people they are, they could be expected to have made a go of their mixed marriage. On the other hand, there is somewhat less assurance about the relationship between Edith, the Protestant mother, and her three Roman Catholic children. This is the realm of subtle, yet pervasive, factors which operate partly above and partly below the level of consciousness. One cannot but wonder, too, about the unspoken reveries of a well-bred woman, living in a family where all other members are of a distinctive other religious persuasion and practice. These are merely questions, raised without prejudice in the case.

The adjustment worked out through the years by Ann and Michael was quite different. Ann came from a wealthy and socially prominent background. Her father was a carefree, adventurous man, devoted to good living, even when its cost exceeded his income. As a result, Ann was left with the slenderest of means after his death. She and her family had been Protestants for many generations, and the particular church to which she was attached was one which befitted her social-class heritage.

Michael came from a good family, too, but it was neither wealthy nor of high-class status, and this was true of Michael. A Catholic by family tradition, he was not very active in meeting his church obligations. Otherwise, he and Ann were well suited, with a number of common interests. An observing friend is sure that there has been a strong physical attraction between the two over the years.

Against the advice of relatives and friends, Ann and Michael were married by a Catholic priest. Ann gave the necessary guarantees, but remained a Protestant. This marriage, celebrated more than thirty years ago, has endured to this date. Six children have been born to this union.

Several aspects of the pattern of adjustment in this case stand out rather clearly. First, for a number of years, Michael and Ann lived in a remote and isolated place. During this time, the family had few social contacts. Michael was occupied with building up his business; Ann, not able to live in the manner that her parents and her former friends had maintained, was content to be a relatively social isolate. Second, not much attention was paid to religious matters during these years. True, the children were baptized as Catholics, but not as soon as the church prescribes. Although the children went to parochial schools, there was little or no religious training in the home.

A third part of the pattern of adjustment came after some eighteen years of marriage. Michael's business having prospered, the family moved from its isolated home to a fashionable suburb of a large city. Changes in both Michael and Ann now began to appear. Michael, grateful for his business success, turned in gratitude to his church, became active in attendance, and interested in its activities. Moreover, he now began to emphasize the religious training of his children, insisting that their entire education be confined to Catholic schools and colleges. For Ann, increased money rekindled the flames of social ambition. She, too, turned to the training of her children with renewed zeal, but such training as is needed to enable them to take their "proper" places in the scheme of things social. Thus a satisfactory compromise evolved—Michael to look after the religious training of the children; Ann, their social careers.

Another compromise achieved by Ann and Michael concerned their separate faiths. Ann has remained a Protestant, with no possibility of change. Michael has told her repeatedly that he would rather have her remain so than to become a poor Catholic, accepting outwardly what she could not believe in her heart. He has trained their Catholic children to respect their mother's honesty and firmness. Ann, on her part, has educated herself to understand Catholicism and the religious duties of her husband and children. She is active in the functions of the Catholic schools to which the children go and the Catholic organizations to which her husband belongs.

What the innermost thoughts of Michael and Ann have been through the years, no one knows. Certainly, there has always been an awareness of the problems which a marriage of this kind creates. On the other hand, tolerance, mutual respect, and intelligent planning and management seem to have gone far in this case to make a successful mixed marriage.

SOME BASIC CONCLUSIONS

The case studies that have been presented, in this and preceding chapters, have been selected to represent types of problems and forms of adjustment which we have found in our studies. It is hoped that readers will identify and regard them as such. Human situations are not like courtroom trials: case histories are used to illustrate, not to indicate finality of judgment. There are, however, certain basic conclusions about mixed marriages that seem apparent, and these will be presented by way of conclusion and summary.

1. Each marriage and each family situation is unique and different from every other one, at least in some respects. There are not, and never can be, two families exactly alike in their inner life. The reason for this is that families are made up of people who are separate individuals, different from each other, and bringing together in the unity of family life an endless variety of combinations. The ways in which individual members of families vary are as numerous as the traits which distinguish them: abilities, disabilities, habits, health, temperament, personality trends, interests, values, age, sex, to name only a few. And the number of

resultant possible combinations defies the imagination. For example, consider a deck of cards. There are fifty-two cards in a deck. And they can be arranged in 2,598,960 different five-card suits. True, there are rules governing the playing of card games, but the particular hand is inevitably separate and distinct. It is so with families. A recognition of this is the first step in a proper approach to any family problem.

2. A mixed marriage adds to the scope and variety of problems in any given case. Some of these are typical, running true to form wherever they appear; others are uniquely individual; many are serious and distressing, others are minor and transitory; there are those that lead directly to the divorce court, others subside into an uneasy equilibrium. But one fact is constant. Even where there is every indication of a successful adjustment, there is a continuing awareness of the situation. One sees persons insisting year after year, for example, that their mixed marriage presents no hazards, and revealing by that very insistence their awareness of them. In other cases, where the solution is by conversion of one to the faith of the other, the new convert is often more ardent in religious profession than the other one, again revealing, through this form of compensatory behavior, that which lies buried beneath the surface. The point emphasized here is this: to pretend that mixed marriages do not bring their own distinctive problems is to belie the facts.

3. The problems of mixed marriages, like those of all marriages, are both changing and persistent. That is to say, the conflicts between the marital partners that grow out of differences in religious backgrounds manifest themselves in changing forms as the years go by. Young people, during the years when most marriages are consummated, do not realize that their marital experiences pass through a sort of natural history. The two preceding chapters have shown

how the problems of marital relations and child rearing
change as mixed marriages proceed.

The idea of the family cycle, developed in connection
with the problems of child rearing in the preceding chapter,
needs re-emphasis here. It is only as one visualizes the various stages in the history of families as they normally tend
to appear that one can appreciate how the families' interests
and problems change, and how deeply ingrained differences
in the cultural values of husband and wife find expression in
the challenge of changing problems. Adjustment of husband-
wife relations in the early years of marriage give way to
questions of child rearing, and later, of child launching.

The long-range point of view in regard to family life cannot be emphasized too strongly. Most of the persons who
contemplate making mixed marriages are young, which
means that they consider only the first stage of the family
cycle, that is, they think in terms of husband-wife relations.
Child rearing—baptism, Sunday school, choice of school—
such matters seem very remote. Youth finds it hard to accept
the inevitability of middle and old age, and to visualize the
problems they bring. Here is where the counsel of older
persons—parents, kinsfolk, pastors, and friends of an older
vintage—can be very helpful. It is no accident that for centuries, the world over, parents and older relatives have controlled or supervised the selection of mates for their sons
and daughters. Certainly their counsel, in so venturesome an
undertaking as a mixed marriage, should be taken into
account.

4. Whatever the possibilities of happiness in mixed marriages, the path to them must ever be through the areas of
understanding, tolerance, compromise, and mutual respect.
Family happiness is not an accident, nor a gift, nor an
incident. It does not come by legislative fiat, priestly bless-

ing, or as a result of the ordering-and-forbidding technique. It is not created by sermons from pulpits or denouncements in the daily press. From these and other sources may come counsel and guidance, inspiration and suggestion, but at best these are but threads which each family can weave into its own fabric as the loom of its daily life shuttles back and forth in the continuing give-and-take of group living. Family happiness is an achievement. It results from effort, intelligent and cooperative effort. Families are happy because they work at it, because they seek consciously and sensibly to promote happiness. The slogan of religious groups that "families that pray together, stay together" might be restated to say that families that can do things together, plan things together, share and enjoy things together, stay together. The key word is "together."

It is against this background that mixed marriages, in the final analysis, must be considered. Once consummated, whatever the difficulties, with these as with other of life's burdens, one must carry them, and move on. And they should be carried, not with the breaking ache of bitterness or the impediment of a crippling paralysis, but in stride as responsibilities which have been assumed, after all, in the freedom of adult choice.

REFERENCES

ADAMS, JAMES TRUSLOW. *The Epic of America.* Boston: Little, Brown & Co., 1943.

BISHOP'S COMMITTEE ON MIXED MARRIAGES. *A Factual Study of Mixed Marriages.* Washington, D.C.: National Catholic Welfare Conference, 1943.

BOARD OF SOCIAL MISSIONS OF THE UNITED LUTHERAN CHURCH IN AMERICA. "A Study of Mixed Marriages in the United Lutheran Church in America."

BOSSARD, JAMES H. S., and ELEANOR STOKER BOLL. *Ritual in Family Living.* Philadelphia: University of Pennsylvania Press, 1950.

——. "The Empathic Complex," *Child Development* (in process of publication).

——. *The Large Family System.* Philadelphia: University of Pennsylvania Press, 1956.

BOSSARD, JAMES H. S., and HAROLD C. LETTS. "Mixed Marriages Involving Lutherans," *Marriage and Family Living* (in process of publication).

CHANCELLOR, LOREN E., and THOMAS P. MONAHAN. "Religious Preference and Interreligious Mixtures in Marriages and Divorces in Iowa," *American Journal of Sociology,* LXI, 3 (November, 1955), 233-39.

FISHBERG, MAURICE. in *Eugenics in Race and State.* Baltimore: Williams & Wilkins Co., 1923.

HANDEL, GERALD, and ROBERT D. HESS. "The Family as an Emotional Organization," *Marriage and Family Living,* XVIII, 2 (May, 1956), 99.

173

KARPF, MAURICE J. "Marriage Counseling and Psychotherapy," *Marriage and Family Living*, XIII, 4 (Fall, 1951), 169-74.

KINSEY, ALFRED C., WARDELL B. POMEROY, CLYDE E. MARTIN, and PAUL H. GEBHARD. *Sexual Behavior in the Human Male*. Philadelphia: W. B. Saunders Co., 1953.

KISER, CLYDE V., and P. K. WHELPTON. "Social and Psychological Factors Affecting Fertility," *Milbank Memorial Fund Quarterly*, XXI, 3 (July, 1943), 226.

———. "Social and Psychological Factors Affecting Fertility," *Milbank Memorial Fund Quarterly*, XXII, 1 (January, 1944), 104.

LANDIS, JUDSON R. "Adjustments After Marriage," *Marriage and Family Living*, IX, 2 (May, 1947), 32-34.

LEIFFER, MURRAY H. "Mixed Marriages and the Children," *The Christian Century*, LXVI, 4 (January 26, 1949), 106-8.

MONAHAN, THOMAS P., and WILLIAM M. KEPHART. "Divorce and Desertion by Religious and Mixed-Religious Groups," *American Journal of Sociology*, LIX, 5 (March, 1954), 454-65.

RESNIK, REUBEN B. "Some Sociological Aspects of Intermarriage of Jew and Non-Jew," *Social Forces*, XII, 1 (October, 1933) 94-102.

SCHNEPP, GERALD J. *Leakage from a Catholic Parish*. Washington, D.C.: Catholic University of America Press, 1942.

———. in Clement S. Mihanovich, Gerald J. Schnepp, and John L. Thomas. *Marriage and the Family* (Milwaukee: Bruce Publishing Co., 1952).

SKIDMORE, REX A., and ANTHON S. CANNON. *Building Your Marriage*. New York: Harper & Bros., 1951.

SLATER, ELIOT, and MOYA WOODSIDE. *Patterns of Marriage*. London: Cassell & Co., Ltd., 1951.

SLOTKIN, J. S. "Jewish-Gentile Intermarriage in Chicago," *American Sociological Review*, VII, 1 (February, 1942), 34-39.

STRAUSS, ANSELM L. "Strain and Harmony in American-Japanese War-Bride Marriages," *Marriage and Family Living*, XVI, 2 (May, 1954), 99-106.

"The Peril of Mixed Marriages," *Literary Digest*, 113, 4 (April 23, 1932).

THOMAS, JOHN L. *The American Catholic Family*. Englewood Cliffs, N.J.: Prentice-Hall, Inc., 1956.

ZIMMERMAN, CARLE C., and CARLFRED B. BRODERICK. "Nature and Role of Informal Family Groups," *Marriage and Family Living,* XVI, 2 (May, 1954), 107-11.

FURTHER READINGS

Barron, Milton L. *People Who Intermarry.* 1946.
Bell, Howard. *Youth Tell Their Story.* 1938.
Landis, Judson T., and Mary G. Landis. *Building A Successful Marriage,* 1948.
Pike, James A. *If You Marry Outside Your Faith.* 1954.
Popenoe, Paul. *Marriage Is What You Make It.* 1950.
Smith, Alson J. *Live All Your Life.* 1955.
Wynn, John C. *Sermons on Marriage and Family Life.* 1956.

Index

177

B